SONGS OF LEONARD COHEN

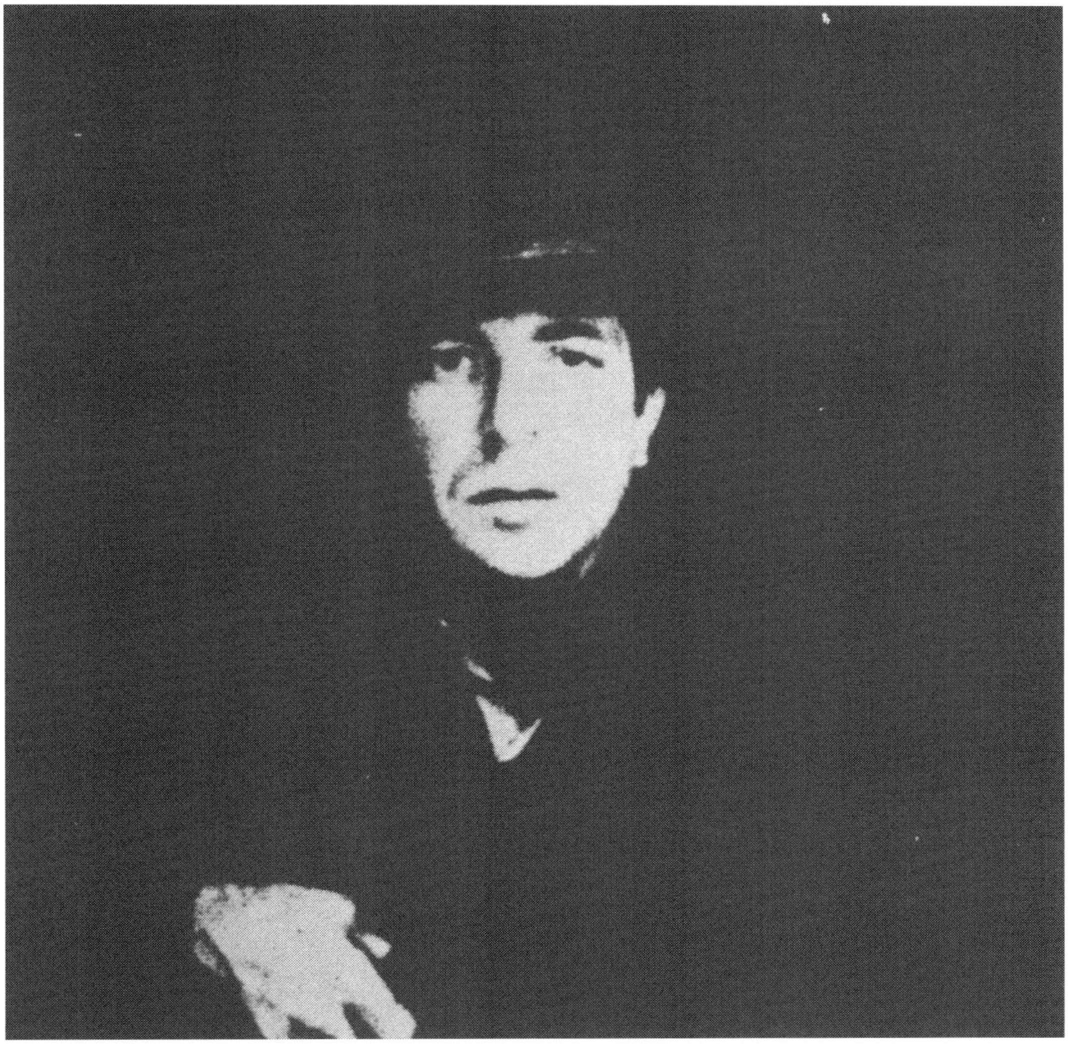

Music Editor: Harvey Vinson
Book Design: Ira Friedlander

HAL•LEONARD®

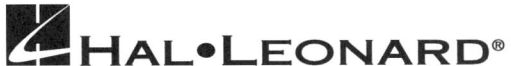

BUCKSKIN BOYS

CONTENTS

37	A Bunch of Lonesome Heroes
34	Bird on the Wire
96	The Butcher
58	Hey, That's No Way to Say Goodbye
88	Lady Midnight
77	Master Song
70	The Old Revolution
62	One of Us Cannot Be Wrong
90	Priests
52	Seems So Long Ago, Nancy
54	Sisters of Mercy
64	So Long, Marianne
44	Stories of the Street
49	Story of Isaac
73	The Stranger Song
40	Suzanne
80	Teachers
83	Tonight Will Be Fine
67	Winter Lady
46	You Know Who I Am

Songs of Leonard Cohen
© 1969 Stranger Music, Inc.

Photographs: Front Cover/Photo by Michael Ochs Archives/Getty Images; Title Page/John Berg; pp. 20, 22, 23, 30 / David Gahr; 21, 32 / Julie Snow; 24, 25 / Roz Kelly; 26, 27, 28 / Michael A. Vaccaro; 32 / James Wigler.

Printed in the EU.

LEONARD COHEN

By WILLIAM KLOMAN

This is pure fantasy. Never heard of the man mentioned here. All good things, Leonard

Leonard Cohen, at 33, is a man-child of our time. A poet-novelist-composer-singer (this is the age of the hyphenate, a sign, some say, that a renaissance is afoot), Cohen has a solid reputation among the young people of his native Canada, where his poems are used by lovers. In America, until recently, he was strictly an underground celebrity. He had written songs for Judy Collins and appeared at the 92d Street Y and was quietly worshipped by a small, scattered band of followers.

Last September, Cohen was featured on "Camera Three," a CBS Sunday morning cultural affairs program. He sang a few songs, read some poems, and was pictured peering sensitively into several tawdry Broadway store windows. The impression he made was strong enough to elicit the greatest audience response in the show's fourteen-year history.

One viewer berated the network for "letting this cancer loose" on the Sabbath, but most of those who wrote wanted to know more about Cohen. Who was this ambiguous and tortured poet who prowled the urban slag dump proclaiming "God is alive. Magic is afoot"?

Cohen's first record album, "Songs of Leonard Cohen," was released recently by Columbia. Cohen sings his poems in a sweet gravelly voice, accompanied only by his own guitar. The words are bitter, the voice is honest, and sales are going very well. Leonard Cohen seems on the verge of becoming a major spokesman for the aging pilgrims of his generation, the so-called "Silent Generation," who came of age under Eisenhower.

The first time I heard Cohen's name was when an otherwise blasé young career woman mentioned meeting him at a party. "I wanted to tell him how much I dug his work," she said. "But I couldn't talk. It was like being introduced to God."

Although he owns a hilltop cottage on the Greek island of Hydra, where he spends most of his time, Cohen's personal pretentions to divinity are strictly limited. On Hydra, Cohen lives with Marianne, the girl he calls "my lady," and their 7-year-old son, Axel. They have no electricity and draw their water from a cistern. In New York, he puts up at the Chelsea or the Henry Hudson Hotel, rarely mixes with the local literateurs, and sometimes spends whole days in front of the mirror trying to figure out where the lines in his face came from.

Cohen's family were well-to-do Montreal merchants. After graduating from McGill University, he took a stab at the family clothing business, but it didn't work out; he chose writing instead. Today, in spite of a small inheritance, his annual income has not yet reached five figures. The recording may change that, but it's not likely to change his gypsy-like style of life. He returns infrequently to Montreal, and only to renew his "neurotic affiliations."

"I've been on the outlaw scene since I was 15," he says. "I had some thing in common with the beatniks, and even more things with the hippies. The next thing may be even closer to where I am."

Where Cohen is is hard to say. Sipping root beer in his frowsy hotel room, the day before his return to Greece, he seems to be a man totally devoid of social defenses. A member of a highly sensitized species whose hope for survival lies in its openness to every shade of human experience. Vulnerability in his art form, and his armor.

"Everybody I meet wipes me out," he says. "Here are all these people plugging away at their roles. *Being* producers and policemen and bishops. It knocks me out, and all I can do is get down on my knees. I don't even think of myself as a writer, singer, or whatever. The occupation of being a man is so much more. In spite of all the philosophical encouragement about hanging loose and all that Sunday school stuff, I admit I'm confused. I can't begin to locate my head. It has a life of its own."

In his first novel, "The Favorite Game," published in 1963, Cohen seemed close to the salvation-through-sex mythos popular among Hemingway's generation. "When I see a woman transformed by the orgasm we have reached together," he wrote, "then I know we've met. Anything else is fiction. That's the vocabulary we speak in today. It's the only language left."

By 1966, when his second novel, "Beautiful Losers," appeared, Cohen's goal was more austere than communication. In "Beautiful Losers," which one critic called "a disagreeable religious epic of incomparable beauty," Cohen was reaching for spiritual perfection through perfect resignation. "What is a saint?" he wrote.

"A saint is someone who has achieved a remote human possibility. It is impossible to say what that possibility is. I think it has something to do with the energy of love. Contact with this energy results in the exercise of a kind of balance in the chaos of existence. A saint does not dissolve the chaos; if he did the world would have changed long ago. I do not think that a saint dissolves the chaos even for himself, for there is something arrogant and warlike in the notion of a man setting the universe in order. It is a kind of balance that is his glory. He rides the drifts like an escaped ski. His course is a caress of the hill....Something in him so loves the world that he gives himself to

the laws of gravity and chance."

Like an escaped ski. A saint, then, is literally someone who is groovy. *With* it. The New Man is clearly light years away from Hemingway's Old Man, battering himself to shreds in a futile struggle against the elements.

"I wish the women would hurry up and take over," Cohen says. "It's going to happen, so let's get it over with. Then we can finally recognize that women really are the minds, and the force that holds everything together, and men really are gossips and artists. Then we could get about our childish work and they could keep the world going. I really am for the matriarchy."

Cohen is willing to embrace any system that might clarify his fate. Which might bring him to the mystical "state of grace" that, for him, means achieving a state of harmony with the rest of creation. Like many of his generation, Cohen yearns for commitment, but no cause is pure enough to claim his loyalty for long.

He's been through drugs, "I Ching," and astrology. He is the only white man on the shadow cabinet of the British Black Muslim leader, Michael X. "Come the revolution," Cohen says, "Michael wants me for permanent adviser to the Ministry of Tourism."

Three years ago Cohen was a strict vegetarian. Today he eats only meat. Dumb animals reproach the carnivore. Radishes scream when they are pulled from the earth. The quest is endless, for there seems no way of existing without injuring our fellow creatures.

Cohen's political temperament is revolutionary. But, like Camus, he is starkly aware of the paradoxes of rebellion. He is frozen in an anarchist's posture, but unable to throw his bomb. At the time of the Bay of Pigs invasion, he went to Havana. He knew it was one of those historical moments that demand action. Once there, however, he was unable to determine on which side to fight. Both sides were evil; both causes were holy.

A tabloid newspaper lies on the bed. Its headline reads, "GREEK KING CALLS FOR REVOLT." Cohen laughs, looking down at it. He shakes his head, eyes closed, and laughs. "It's *too much*," he says. "It breaks me up." But somehow revolutionary kings seem appropriate in Leonard Cohen's world.

"People ask me why I didn't stand up and fight for the Papandreou Government, since I was living in Greece and supposedly enjoying the fruits of democracy," Cohen says. "But I wonder where Melina and the others would be if it had been a *royalist* coup that overthrew Papandreou. The rebels were colonels — petit bourgeois. After the coup an old lady of an aristocratic family said to me, 'We don't *know* any of these people.' That was her comment on the so-called death of Greek democracy. When it comes down to power, it's always 'them' and 'us.' The rest is just a cover story, and I'm not interested in cover-stories. I have a friend who was tortured for six hours by the Papandreou police on a minor charge which they later dropped. 'Don't be angry,' they told him. 'We just have black hearts.'"

Cohen sympathizes with the protest movement in America, but fears the organization-minded mobilizers among the rebels. In one of the songs on his new album he speaks to the revolutionaries:

*I know you've heard it's over,
And war must surely come.
The cities they are broke in half,
And the middle-men are gone.
But let me ask you one more time,
Oh, children of the dust:
All these hunters who are shrieking now,
Oh, do they speak for us?*

"The American dream is very much on everybody's mind these days," Cohen tells a visitor at the Henry Hudson. "The Whitman dream. The Jefferson dream. The people who mobilize protests in the streets—they're patriots. That's why it's difficult to resist them.

"Look. My novels have a very pathological tone. They attract letters from people in pain. What I find out from my mail, from my friends, from everywhere, is that the best products of our time are in agony. The finest sensibilities of the age are convulsed with pain. That means a change is at hand.

"The status quo people know it. They know it from the way young people dress. When people start to wear different clothes, God knows what can happen. They see the new fashions and they say, 'What are you *doing* to us?' It's all right to have odd opinions, but when you start to dress differently, you've mobilized.

"Of course it's a revolution. But I want to see the *real* revolution. I don't want it siphoned off by the mobilization people. It's got to take place in every room. Revolutionaries, in their heart of hearts, are excited by the tyranny they wield. The lines are being drawn and people on both sides are beginning to terrorize each other. Somehow we have to break out of this process, which can only lead to both sides becoming *like* each other. I'm afraid that when the Pentagon is finally stormed and taken, it will be by guys wearing uniforms very much like the ones worn by the guys defending it."

Cohen walks to the window and stands watching a ship pass, far below, on the Hudson. A verse from one of his songs springs to mind:
*I lean from my window sill
In this old hotel I chose.
One hand on my suicide,
And one hand on the rose.*

Will he jump? And if he does, will he be buoyed up by the breeze, in a midwinter miracle of levitation? The tensions of his spiritual balancing act make all things seem possible. He turns from the window and finds his voice again.

"The thing we find unpalatable about the law," he says, "is that it is there to protect property, not the spirit. It is no longer holy. We rebel. But what we've been calling a revolution we should call a return. As soon as the old law is dead — as soon as everything becomes possible—you suddenly learn the necessity for law. Things have to be placed in order again. So we will have to write a new law. One which is meaningful to us. A very pedestrian law about how to behave with one another.

"People keep saying India, India, India. But the Indian vocabulary is much too precise for us. Our natural vocabularly is Judeo-Christian. That is our blood-myth. We have to rediscover law from inside our own heritage, and we have to rediscover the crucifixion. The crucifixion will again be understood as a universal symbol, not as just an experiment in sadism or masochism or arrogance. It will have to be rediscovered because that's where man is at. On the cross."

© 1968 by The New York Times Company. Reprinted by permission.

GREECE

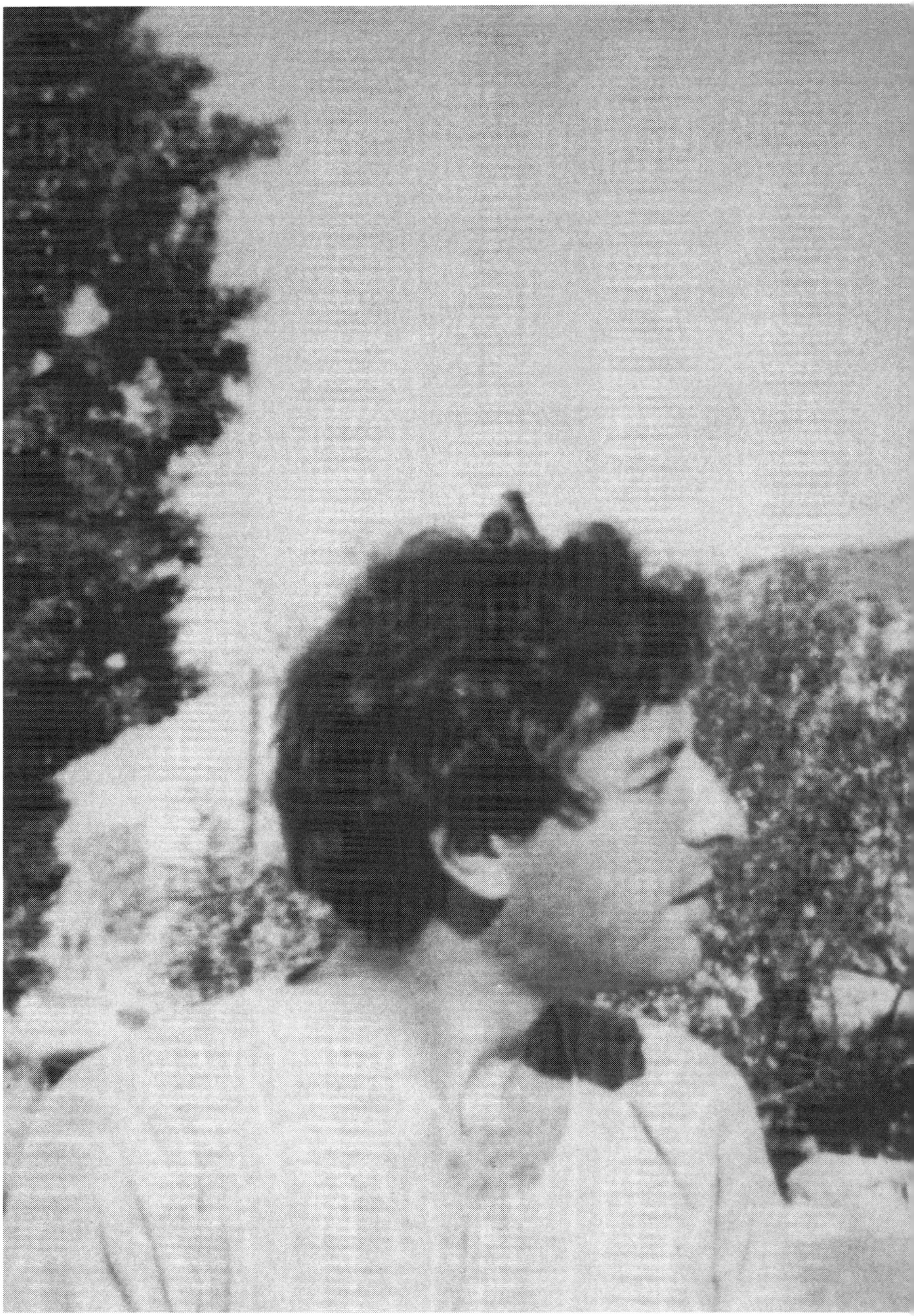

MARIANNE

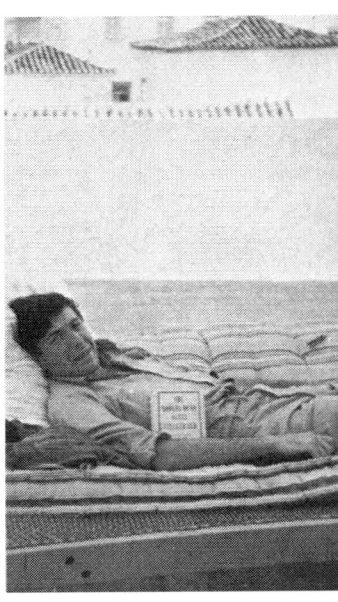

11

AXEL

MARIANNE

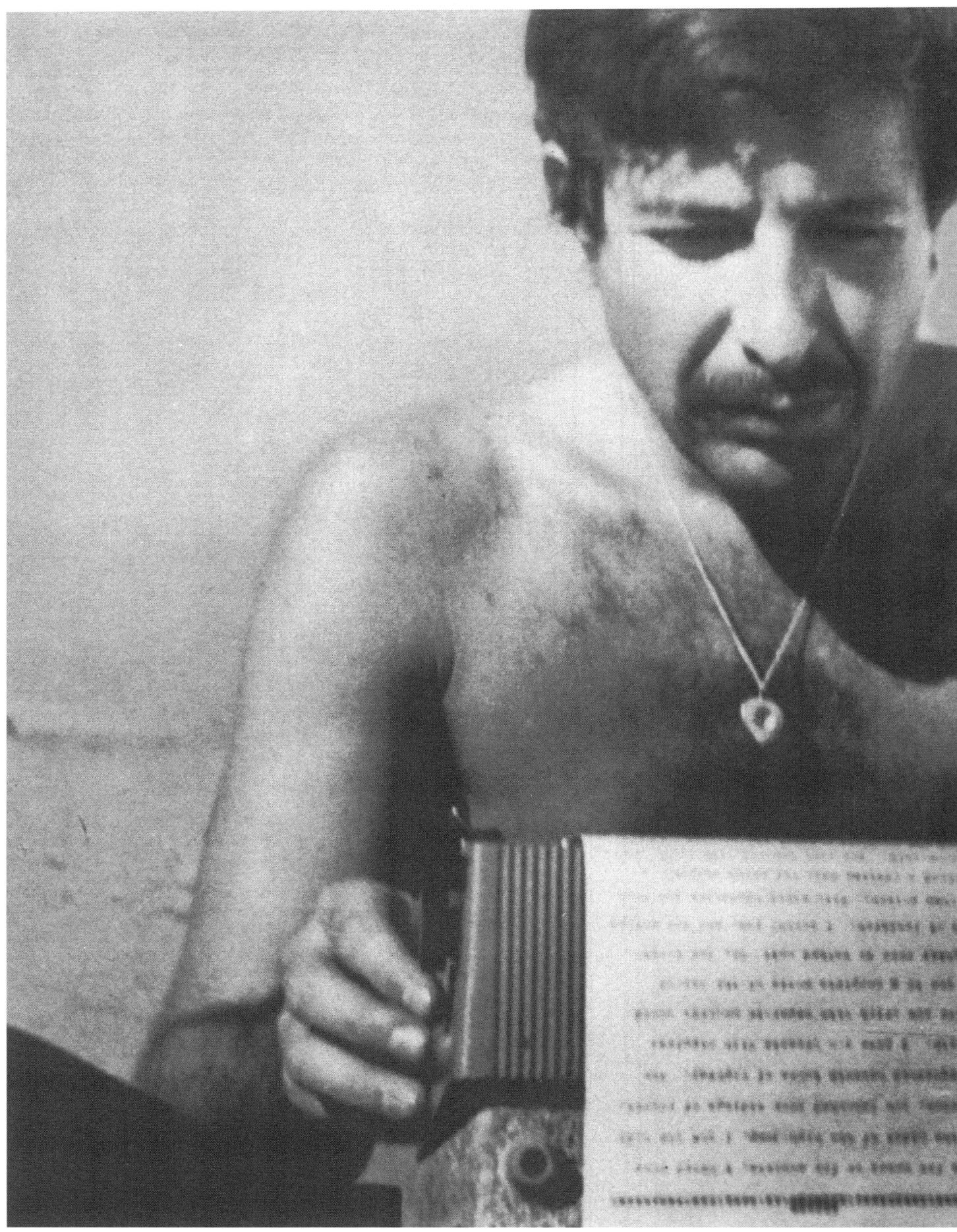

JUDY COLLINS

NASHVILLE

JOHN HAMMOND

JUDY COLLINS

SONGS OF LEONARD COHEN

The guitar accompaniment for each song is clearly illustrated in easy to read tablature. The tablature system is based on a combination of the French and English systems. Each of the six lines in the tablature staff represents a corresponding guitar string.

Tablature   Guitar Strings

←highest sounding

← lowest sounding

Arabic numbers appearing on the tablature lines indicate various fretting positions for the left hand. For example, an "o" on the top line of the tablature staff indicates that you play the highest sounding string unfingered by the left hand.

A "1" on the top line indicates that you play the highest sounding string fingered at the 1st fret:

An entire C chord looks like this in tablature:

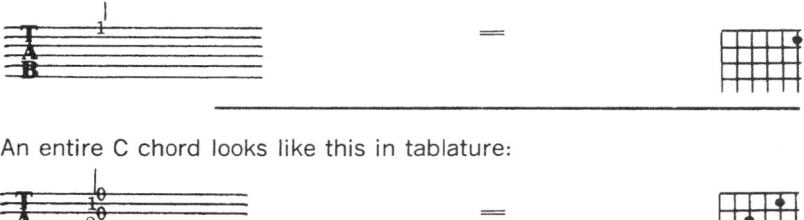

Chord boxes above the music pictorially illustrate the left hand fingering. Do not play the strings indicated by broken lines when you strum the chord. In this D chord you would not play the lowest sounding string.

D Chord

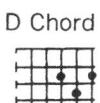

The abbreviations *i, m,* and *r* are used to indicate the index, middle, and ring fingers of the right hand. Notes with their stems pointing down are to be played with the right hand thumb.

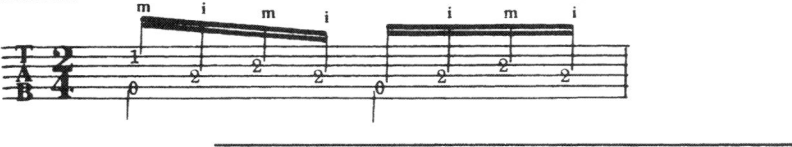

For note readers, the guitar accompaniment for the song *Hey, That's No Way To Say Goodbye* is notated in tablature as well as the corresponding music notes. This clearly illustrates the transference of music notes into tablature.

BIRD ON THE WIRE

Words & Music by Leonard Cohen

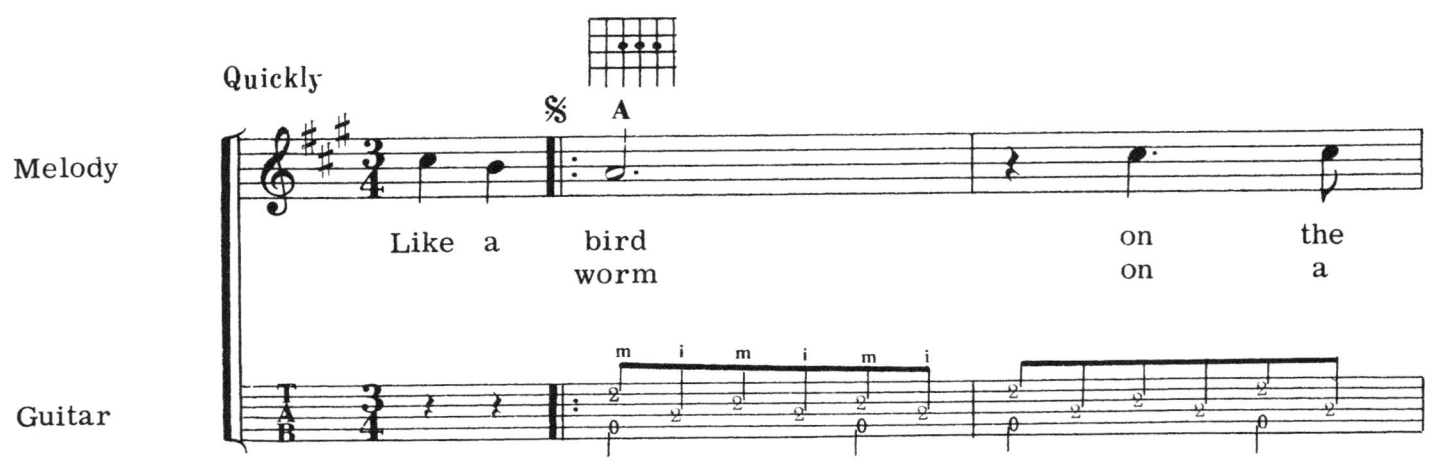
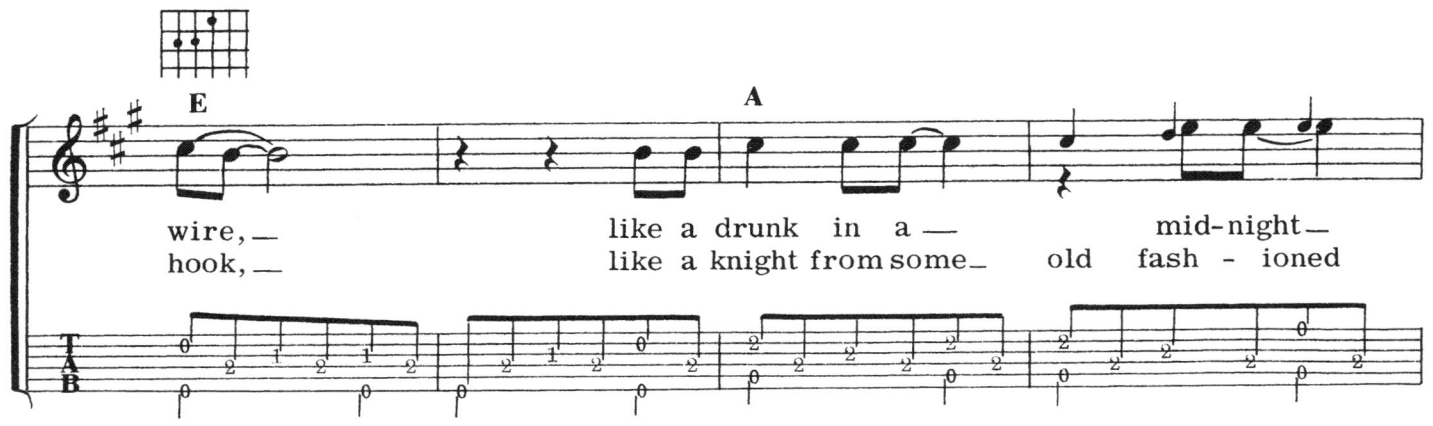

© Copyright 1968 Sony/ATV Songs LLC, USA.
Chrysalis Songs Limited.
All Rights Reserved. International Copyright Secured.

Like a bird on the wire
Like a drunk in a midnight choir
I have tried in my way to be free
Like a worm on a hook
Like a knight from some old-fashioned book
I have saved all my ribbons for thee
    If I have been unkind
    I hope that you can just let it go by
    If I have been untrue,
    I hope you know it was never to you.

Like a baby stillborn
Like a beast with his horn
I have torn everyone who reached out for me
But I swear by this song
And by all that I have done wrong
I will make it all up to thee.
    I saw a beggar leaning on his wooden crutch
    He said to me, "You must not ask for so much."
    And a pretty woman leaning in her darkened door,
    She cried to me, "Hey, why not ask for more?"

A Bunch Of Lonesome Heroes

Words & Music by Leonard Cohen

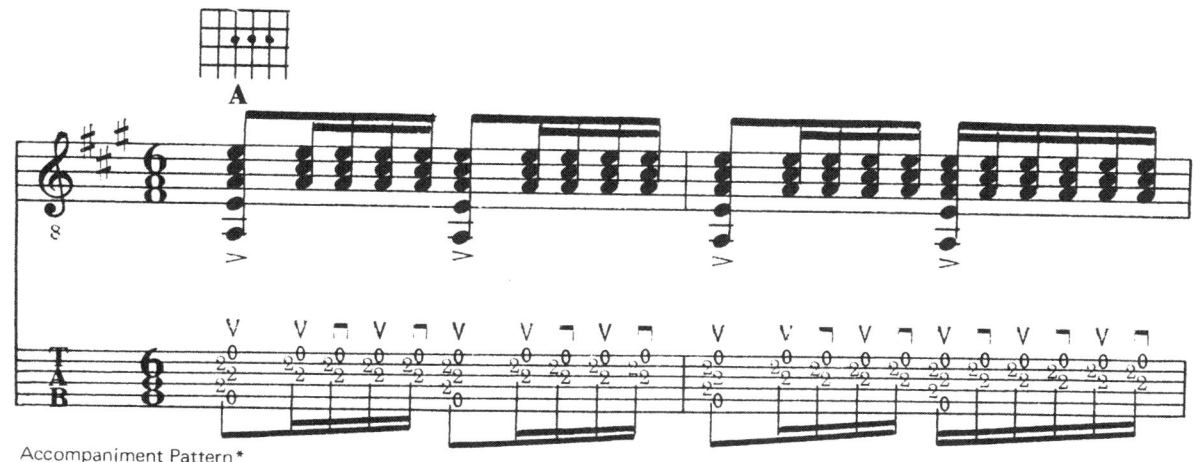

Accompaniment Pattern*

Quickly

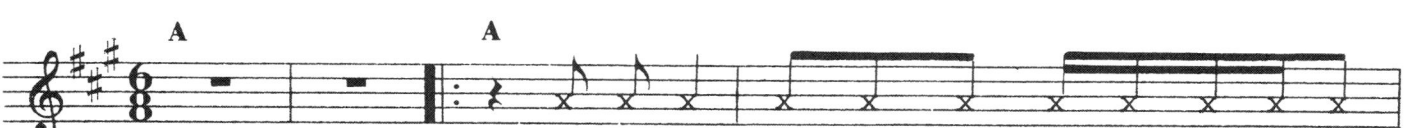

A bunch of lone-some and ver-y quar-rel-some

The x's on the staff indicate that the words are to be spoken rather than sung.

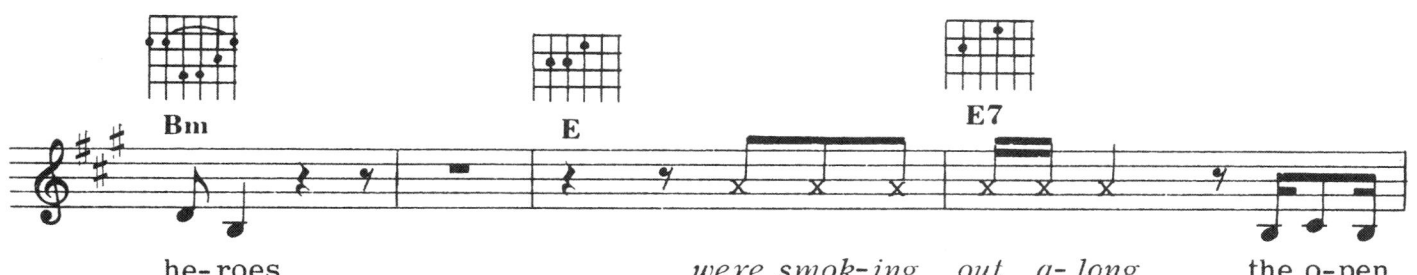

he-roes   were smok-ing out a-long   the o-pen

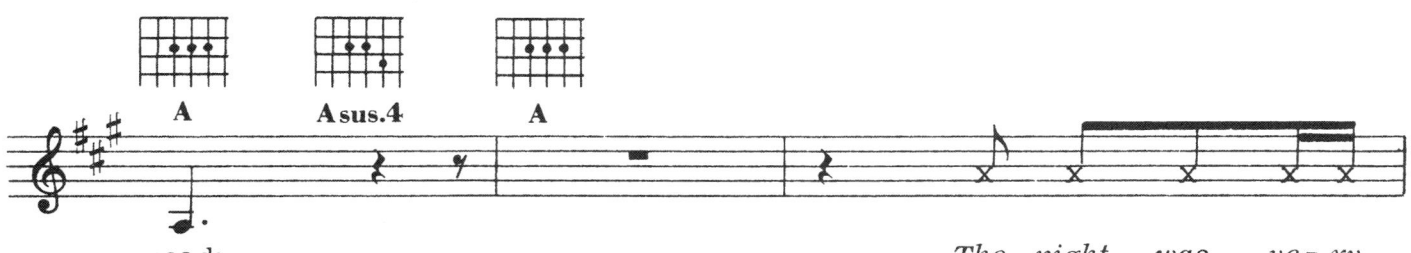

road;   The night was ve-ry

dark and thick be-tween them,   each man be -

*A two bar rhythmic phrase with beats "1" and "4" accented.

© Copyright 1969 Sony/ATV Songs LLC, USA.
Chrysalis Music Limited.
All Rights Reserved. International Copyright Secured.

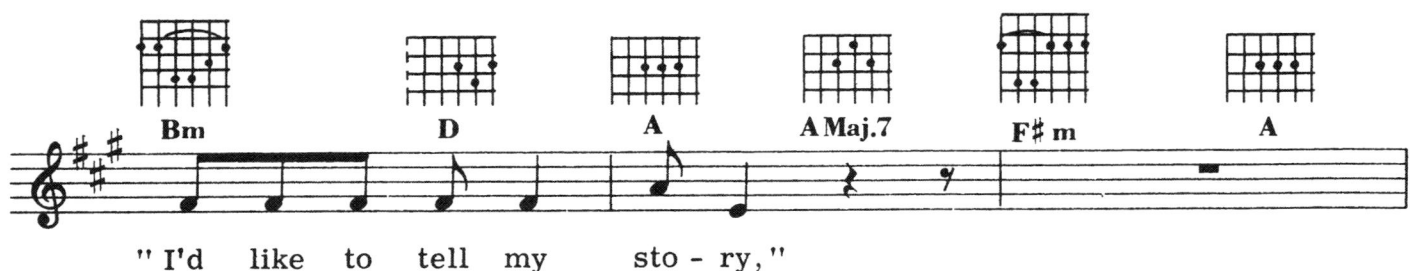

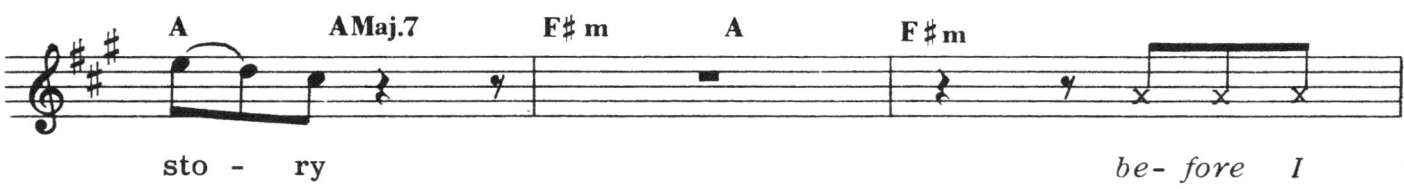
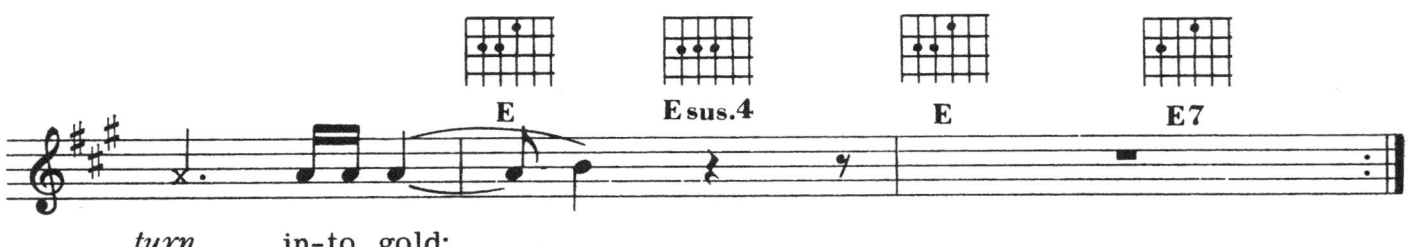

A BUNCH OF LONESOME HEROES

A bunch of lonesome and very quarrelsome heroes
Were smoking out along the open road;
The night was very dark and thick between them
Each man beneath his ordinary load.
    "I'd like to tell my story,"
    Said one of them so young and bold;
    "I'd like to tell my story,
    Before I turn to gold."

But no one really could hear him,
The night so dark and thick and green;
Well, I guess that these heroes must always live there
Where you and I have only been.
    Put out your cigarette, my love,
    You've been alone too long;
    And some of us are very hungry now
    To hear what it is you've done that was so wrong.

I sing this for the crickets
I sing this for the army
I sing this for your children
And for all who do not need me.
    "I'd like to tell my story,"
    Said one of them so bold;
    I'd like to tell my story
    'cause you know I feel I'm turning into gold."

Suzanne

Words & Music by Leonard Cohen

© Copyright 1966 Sony/ATV Songs LLC, USA.
TRO Essex Music Limited.
All Rights Reserved. International Copyright Secured.

Suzanne takes you down
To her place near the river
You can hear the boats go by
You can spend the night beside her.
And you know that she's half crazy
But that's why you want to be there
And she feeds you tea and oranges
That come all the way from China.
And just when you mean to tell her
That you have no love to give her
Then she gets you on her wavelength
And she lets the river answer
That you've always been her lover
And you want to travel with her
And you want to travel blind
And you know that she will trust you
For you've touched her perfect body
    with your mind.

And Jesus was a sailor
When he walked upon the water
And he spent a long time watching
From his lonely wooden tower.
And when he knew for certain
Only drowning men could see him
He said, "All men will be sailors then
Until the sea shall free them."

But he himself was broken
Long before the sky would open
Forsaken, almost human,
He sank beneath your wisdom like a stone.
And you want to travel with him
And you want to travel blind
And you think maybe you'll trust him
For he's touched your perfect body
    with his mind.

Now Suzanne takes your hand
And she leads you to the river
She is wearing rags and feathers
From Salvation Army counters.
And the sun pours down like honey
On our lady of the harbour;
And she shows you where to look
Among the garbage and the flowers.
There are heroes in the seaweed,
There are children in the morning,
They are leaning out for love
And they will lean that way forever.
While Suzanne holds the mirror
And you want to travel with her
And you want to travel blind
And you know that you can trust her
For she's touched your perfect body
    with her mind.

Stories Of The Street

Words & Music by Leonard Cohen

44

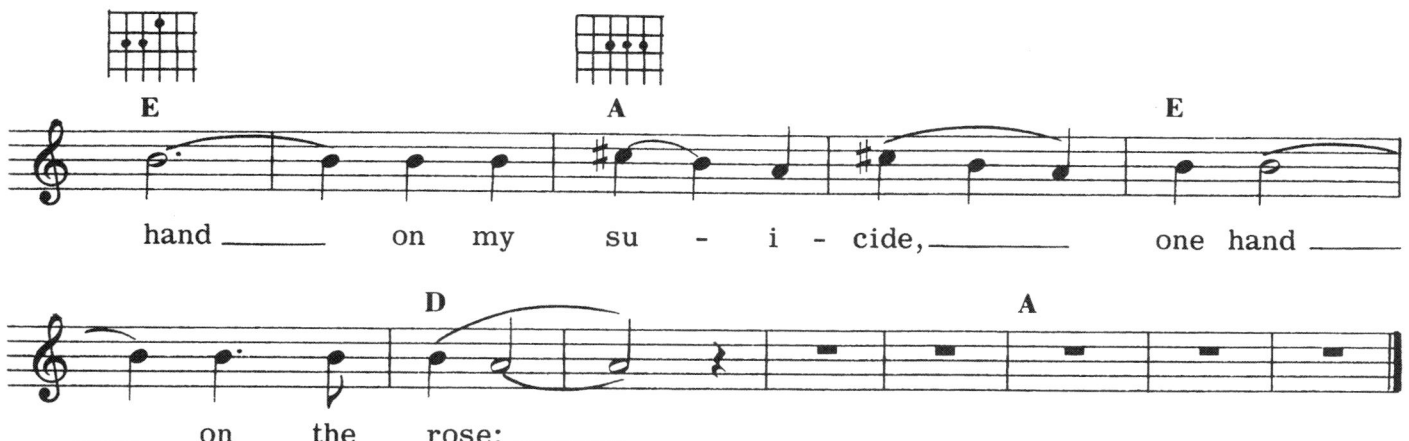

hand ___ on my su-i-cide, ___ one hand ___ on the rose; ___

The stories of the street are mine
The Spanish voices laugh
The Cadillacs go creeping down
Through the night and the poison gas.
I lean from my window sill
In this old hotel I chose
One hand on my suicide
One hand on the rose.

I know you've heard it's over now
And war must surely come
The cities they are broke in half
And the middle men are gone.
But let me ask you one more time
O, children of the dust,
All these hunters who are shrieking now
Do they speak for us?

And where do all these highways go
Now that we are free?
Why are the armies marching still
That were coming home to me?
O, lady with your legs so fine
O, stranger at your wheel
You are locked into your suffering
And your pleasures are the seal

The age of lust is giving birth
And both the parents ask
The nurse to tell them fairy tales
On both sides of the glass
Now the infant with his cord
Is hauled in like a kite
And one eye filled with blueprints
One eye filled with night.

O, come with me my little one
And we will find that farm
And grow us grass and apples there
And keep all the animals warm.
And if by chance I wake at night
And I ask you who I am
O, take me to the slaughter house
I will wait there with the lamb.

With one hand on a hexagram
And one hand on a girl
I balance on a wishing well
That all men call the world.
We are so small between the stars
So large against the sky
And lost among the subway crowds
I try to catch your eye.

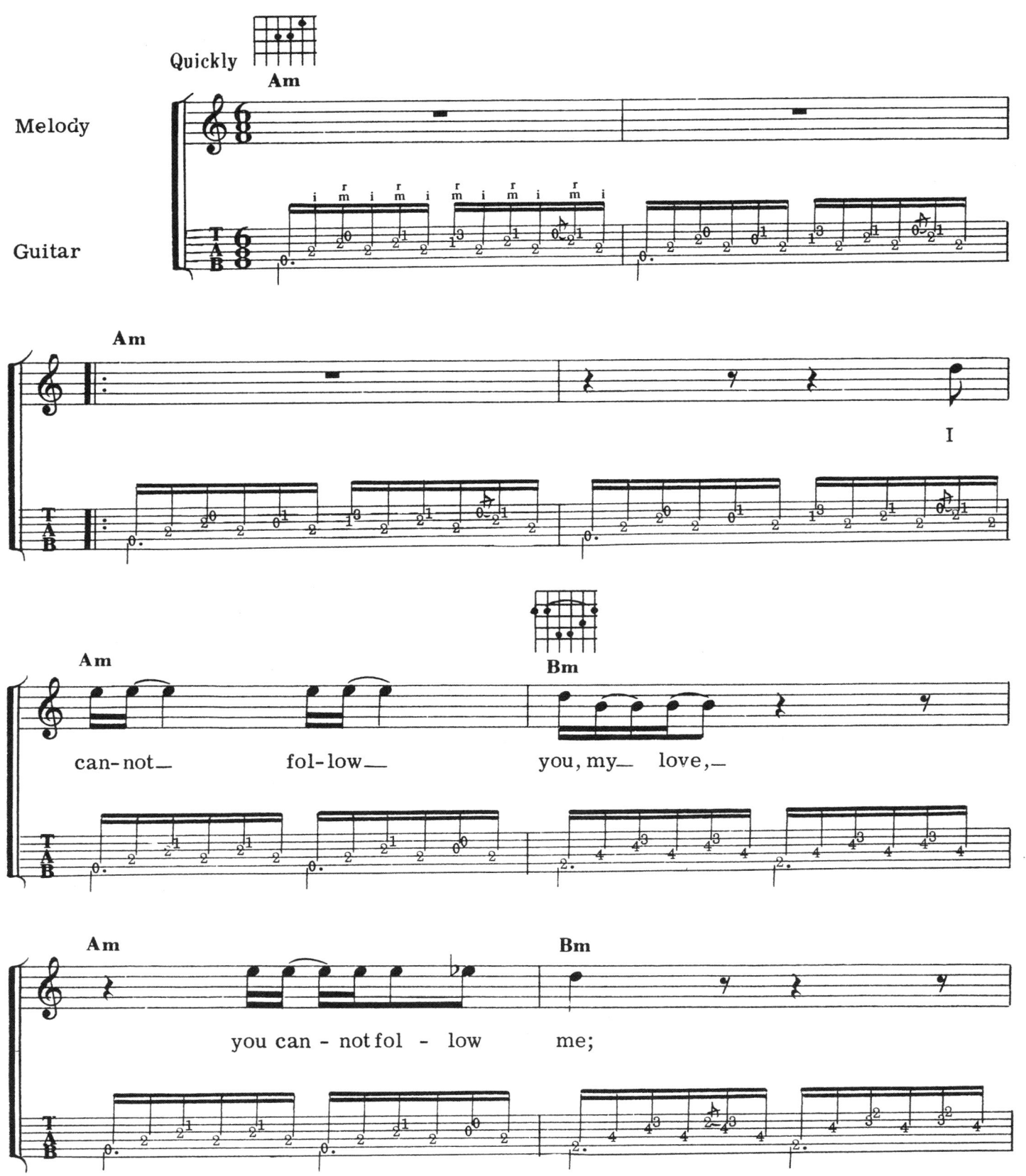

I cannot follow you my love
You cannot follow me
I am the distance you put between
All of the moments that we will be.

Chorus:
You know who I am
You've stared at the sun
Well I am the one who loves
Changing from nothing to one.

Sometimes I need you naked
Sometimes I need you wild
I need you to carry my children in
And I need you to kill a child.

Chorus

If you should ever track me down
I will surrender there
And I'll leave with you one broken man
Whom I'll teach you to repair.

Chorus

I cannot follow you my love
You cannot follow me
I am the distance you put between
All of the moments that we will be.

Chorus (and Coda)

Story of Isaac

Words & Music by Leonard Cohen

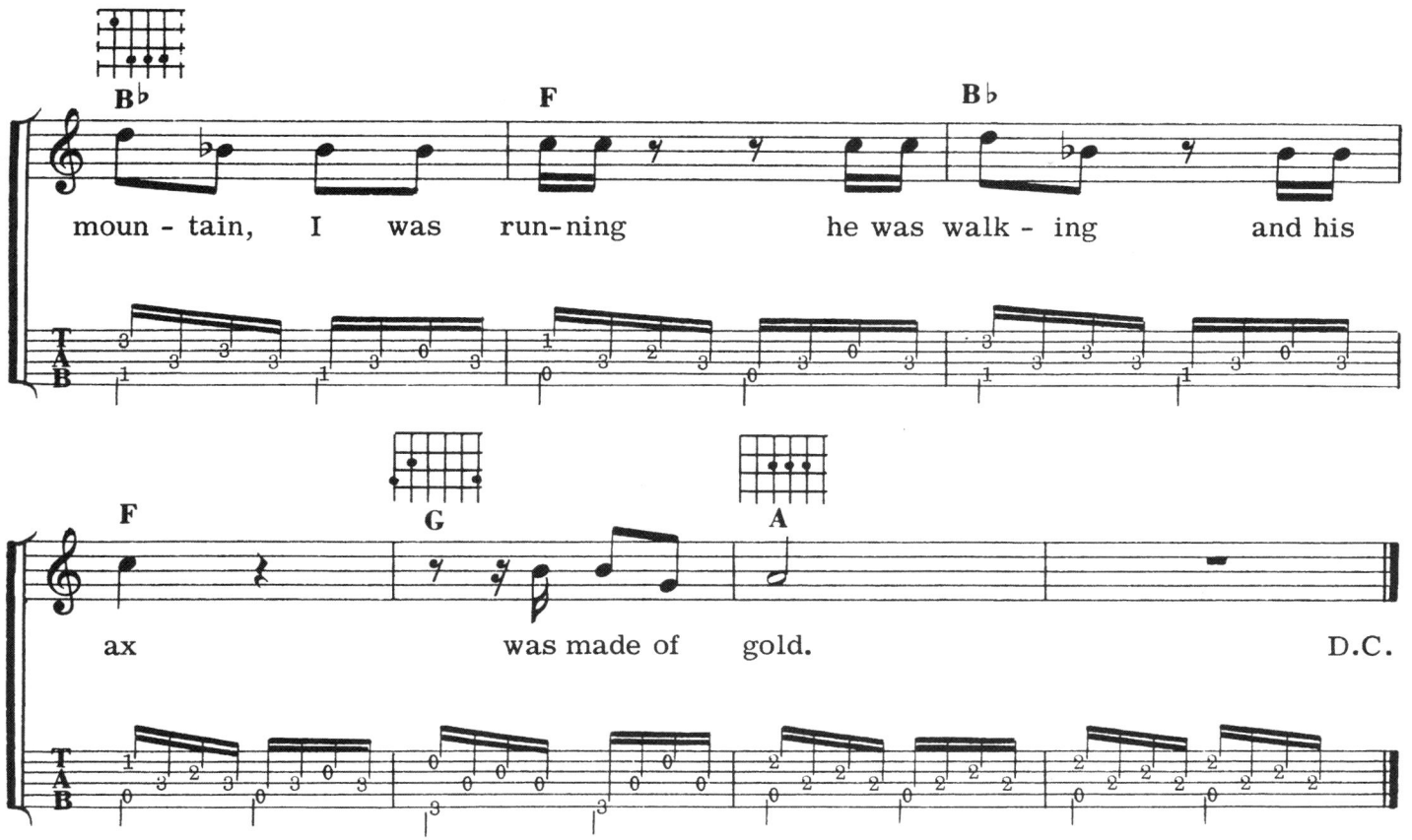

The door it opened slowly
   My father he came in
   I was nine years old
And he stood so tall above me
   Blue eyes they were shining
   And his voice was very cold.
Said, "I've had a vision
   And you know I'm strong and holy
   I must do what I've been told."
So he started up the mountain
   I was running he was walking
   And his ax was made of gold.

The trees they got much smaller
   The lake a lady's mirror
   We stopped to drink some wine
Then he threw the bottle over
   Broke a minute later
   And he put his hand on mine.
Thought I saw an eagle
   But it might have been a vulture,
   I never could decide.
Then my father built an altar
   He looked once behind his shoulder
   He knew I would not hide.

You who build the altars now
   To sacrifice these children
   You must not do it any more.
A scheme is not a vision
   And you never have been tempted
   By a demon or a god.
You who stand above them now
   Your hatchets blunt and bloody,
   You were not there before.
When I lay upon a mountain
   And my father's hand was trembling
   With the beauty of the word.

And if you call me brother now
   Forgive me if I inquire
   Just according to whose plan?
When it all comes down to dust
   I will kill you if I must
   I will help you if I can.
When it all comes down to dust
   I will help you if I must
   I will kill you if I can.
And mercy on our uniform
Man of peace or man of war —
   The peacock spreads his fan.

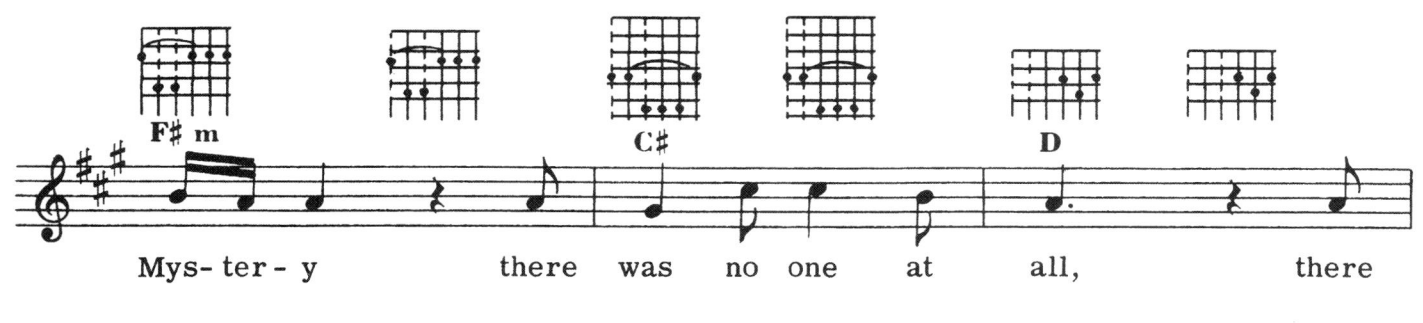

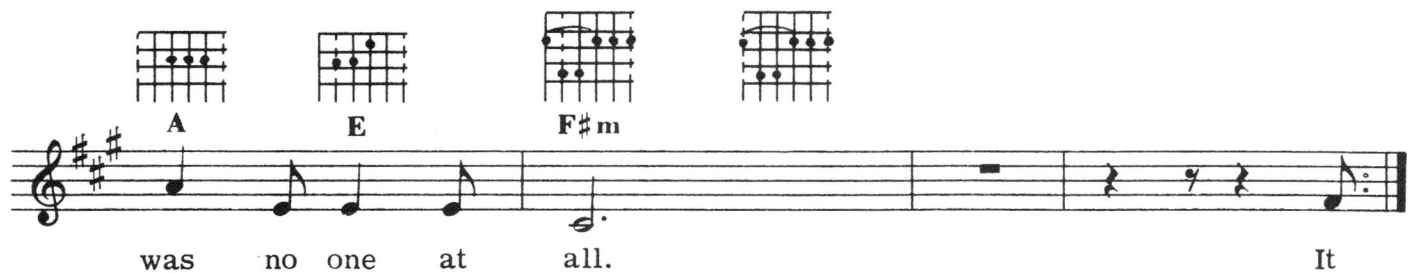

It seems so long ago
   Nancy was alone
Looking at The Late Late Show
   through a semi-precious stone.
In the House of Honesty
   her father was on trial
In the House of Mystery
   there was no one at all
   there was no one at all.

It seems so long ago
   none of us were strong
Nancy wore green stockings
   and she slept with everyone.
She never said she'd wait for us
   although she was alone
I think she fell in love for us
   in nineteen sixty-one
   in nineteen sixty-one.

It seems so long ago
   Nancy was alone
A forty-five beside her head
   an open telephone.
We told her she was beautiful
   we told her she was free
But none of us would meet her in
   the House of Mystery
   the House of Mystery.

And now you look around you
   see her everywhere
Many use her body
   many comb her hair.
And in the hollow of the night
   when you are cold and numb
You hear her talking freely then
   she's happy that you've come
   she's happy that you've come.

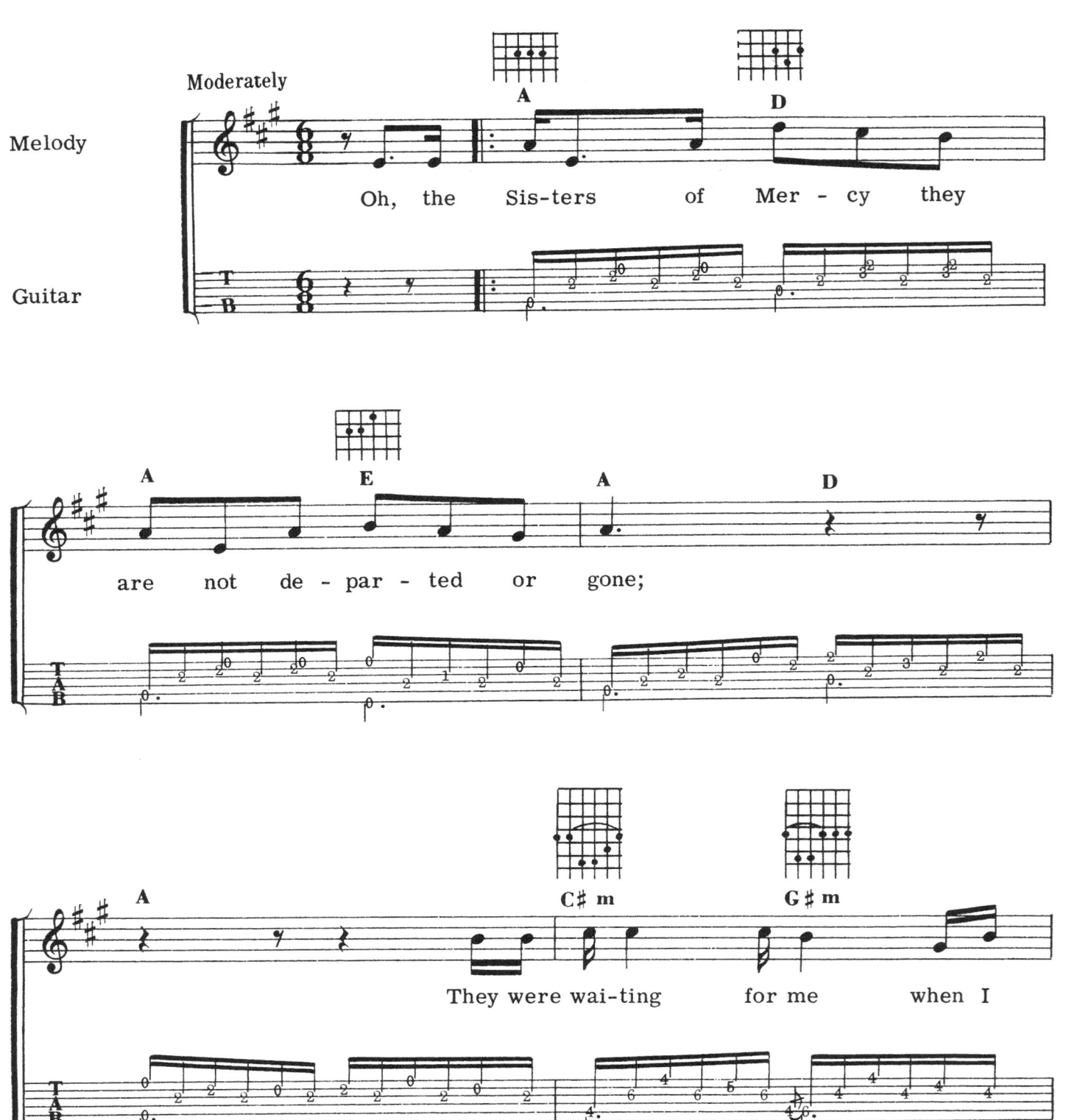

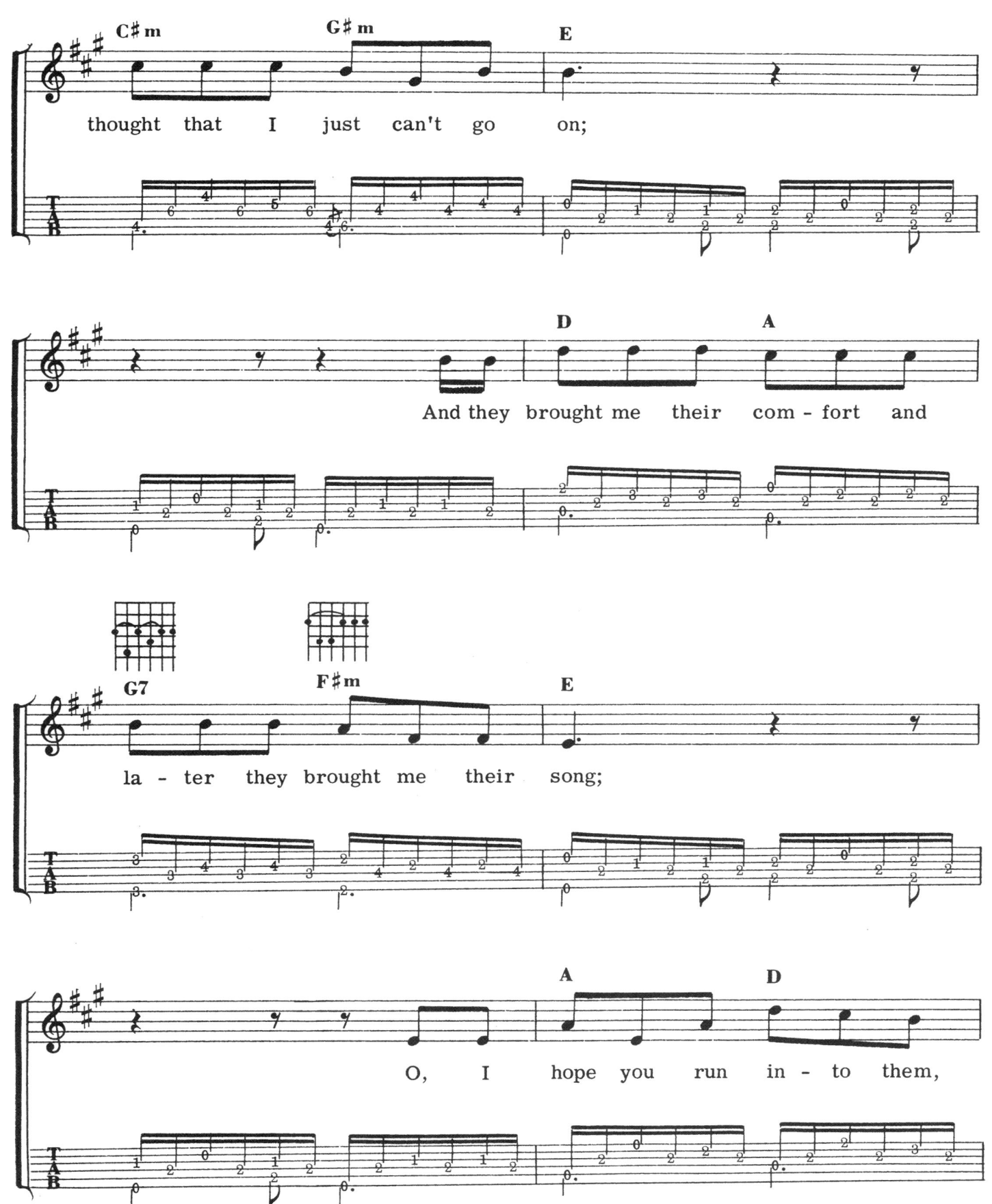

SISTERS OF MERCY

Oh, the Sisters of Mercy
They are not departed or gone
They were waiting for me
When I thought that I just can't go on
And they brought me their comfort
And later they brought me their song
O, I hope you run into them
You who've been traveling so long.

Yes, you who must leave everything
That you cannot control
It begins with your family
But soon it comes round to your soul.
Well, I've been where you're hanging
I think I can see how you're pinned
When you're not feeling holy
Your loneliness says that you've sinned.

They lay down beside me
I made my confession to them
They touched both my eyes
And I touched the dew on their hem.
If your life is a leaf
That the seasons tear off and condemn
They will bind you with love
That is graceful and green as a stem.

When I left they were sleeping
I hope you run into them soon.
Don't turn on the lights,
You can read their address by the moon;
And you won't make me jealous
If I hear that they sweetened your night
We weren't lovers like that
And besides it would still be all right
We weren't lovers like that
And besides it would still be all right.

HEY, THAT'S NO WAY TO SAY GOODBYE

Words & Music by Leonard Cohen

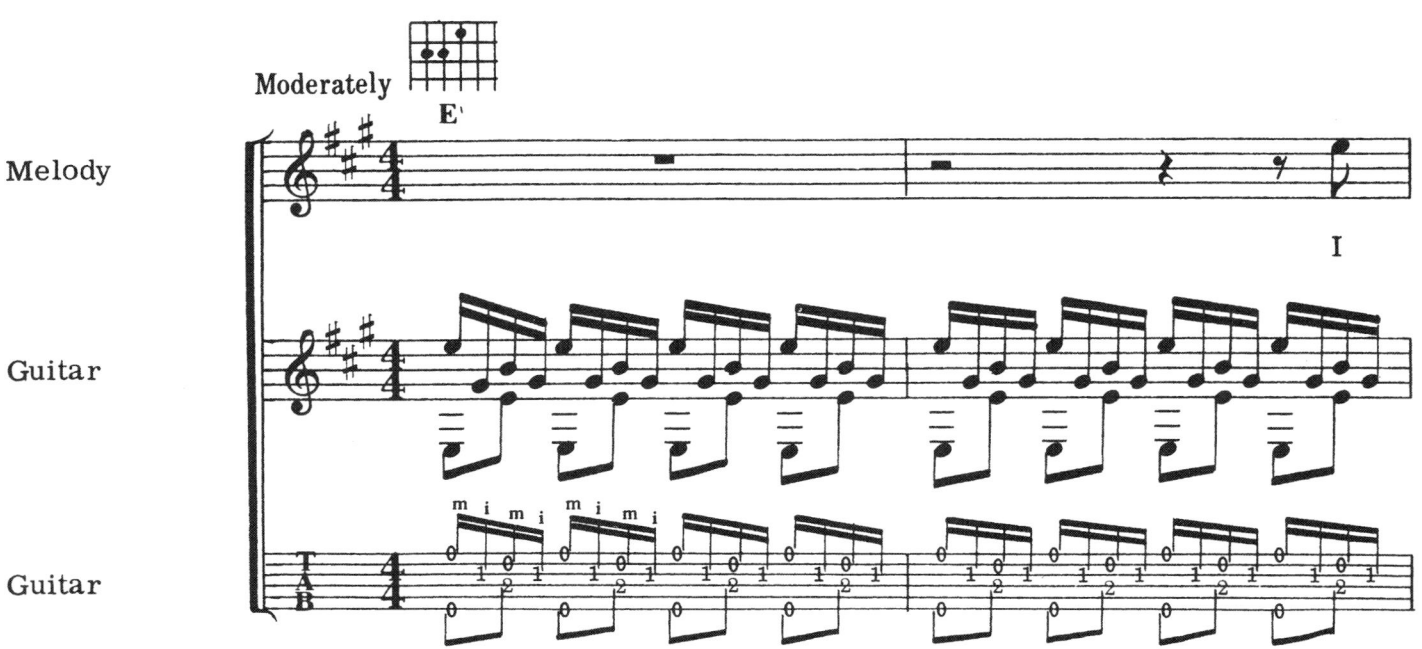

I loved you in the morn - ing, our kiss - es sweet and warm,___ your

© Copyright 1967 Sony/ATV Songs LLC, USA.
Chrysalis Songs Limited.
All Rights Reserved. International Copyright Secured.

I loved you in the morning
Our kisses sweet and warm
Your hair upon the pillow
Like a sleepy golden storm.
Yes, many loved before us
I know that we are not new
In city and in forest
They smiled like me and you.
But now it's come to distances
And both of us must try
Your eyes are soft with sorrow
Hey, that's no way to say goodbye.

I'm not looking for another
As I wander in my time
Walk me to the corner
Our steps will always rhyme.
You know my love goes with you
As your love stays with me
It's just the way it changes
Like the shoreline and the sea.
But let's not talk of love or chains
And things we can't untie,
Your eyes are soft with sorrow,
Hey, that's no way to say goodbye.

I loved you in the morning
Our kisses deep and warm
Your hair upon the pillow
Like a sleepy golden storm.
Yes, many loved before us
I know that we are not new
In city and in forest
They smiled like me and you.
But let's not talk of love or chains
And things we can't untie,
Your eyes are soft with sorrow
Hey, that's no way to say goodbye.

ONE OF US CAN NOT BE WRONG

Words & Music by Leonard Cohen

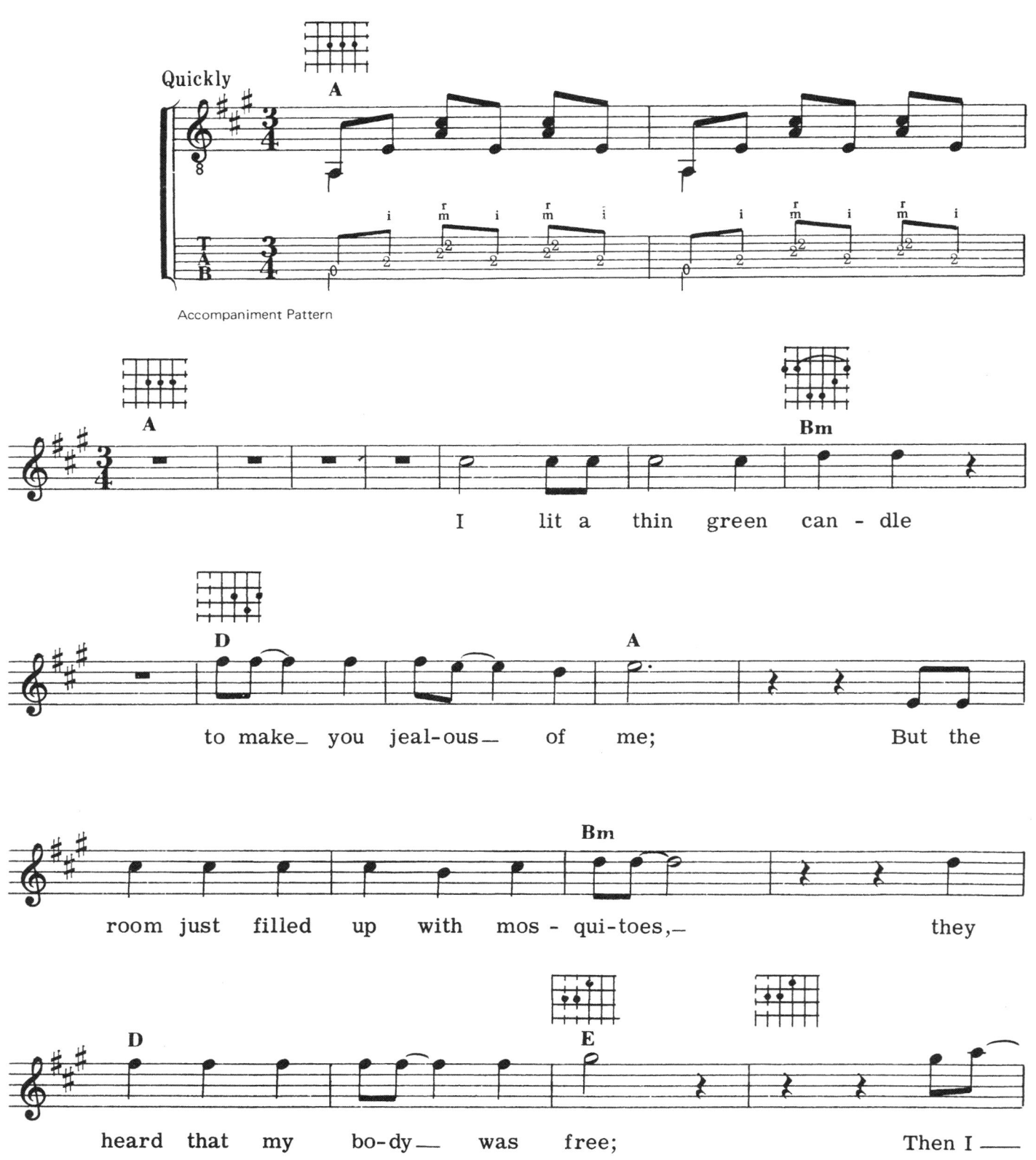

I lit a thin green candle
To make you jealous of me
But the room just filled up with mosquitoes
They heard that my body was free.
Then I took the dust of a long sleepless night
And I put it in your little shoe
And then I confess that I tortured the dress
That you wore for the world to look through.

I showed my heart to the doctor
He said I'd just have to quit
Then he wrote himself a prescription
And your name was mentioned in it.
Then he locked himself in a library shelf
With the details of our honeymoon
And I hear from the nurse
That he's gotten much worse
And his practice is all in a ruin.

I heard of a saint who had loved you
I studied all night in his school
He taught that the duty of lovers
Is to tarnish the golden rule.
And just when I was sure
That his teachings were pure
He drowned himself in the pool
His body is gone but back here on the lawn
His spirit continues to drool.

An Eskimo showed me a movie
He'd recently taken of you
The poor man could hardly stop shivering,
His lips and his fingers were blue.
I suppose that he froze
When the wind took your clothes
And I guess he just never got warm
But you stand there so nice in your blizzard of ice
O, please let me come into the storm.

SO LONG, MARIANNE

Words & Music by Leonard Cohen

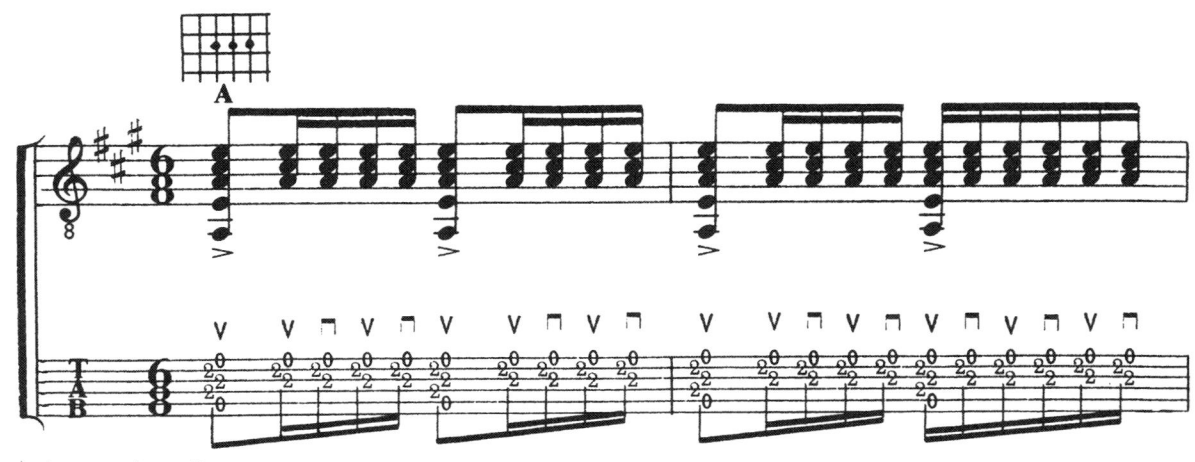

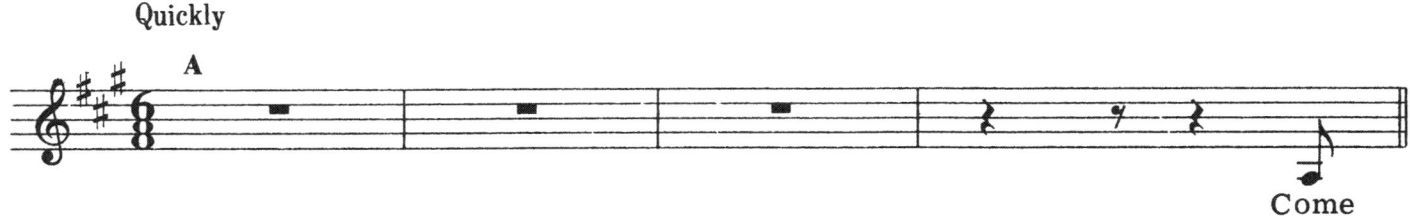

© Copyright 1967 Sony/ATV Songs LLC, USA.
Chrysalis Songs Limited.
All Rights Reserved. International Copyright Secured.

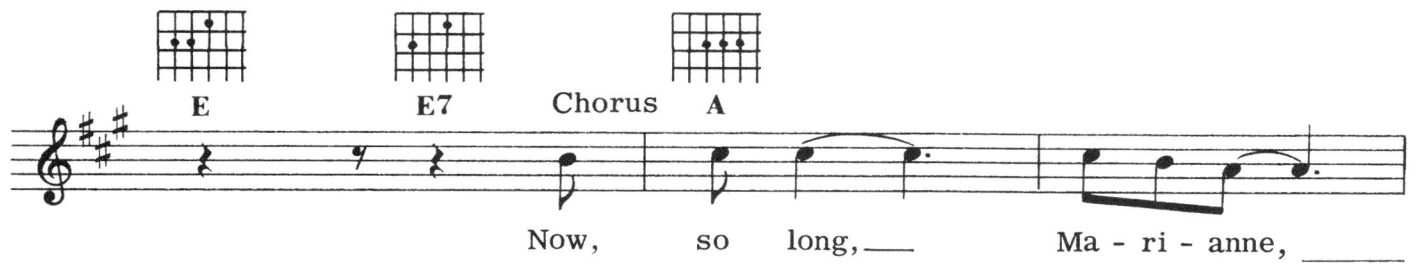

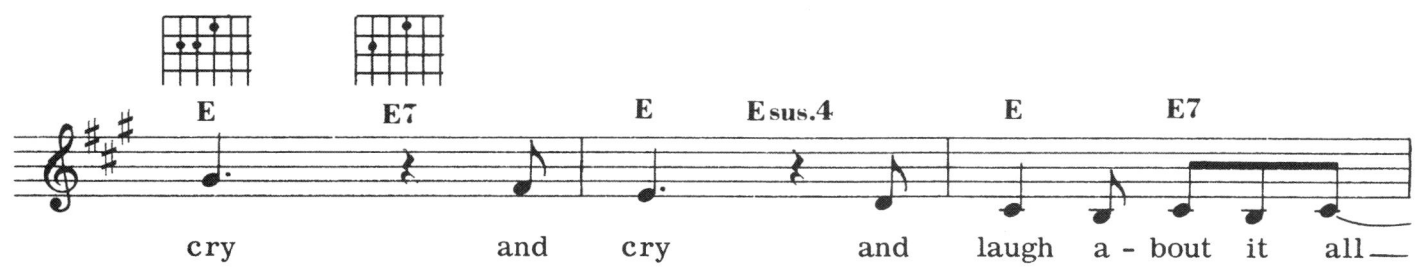

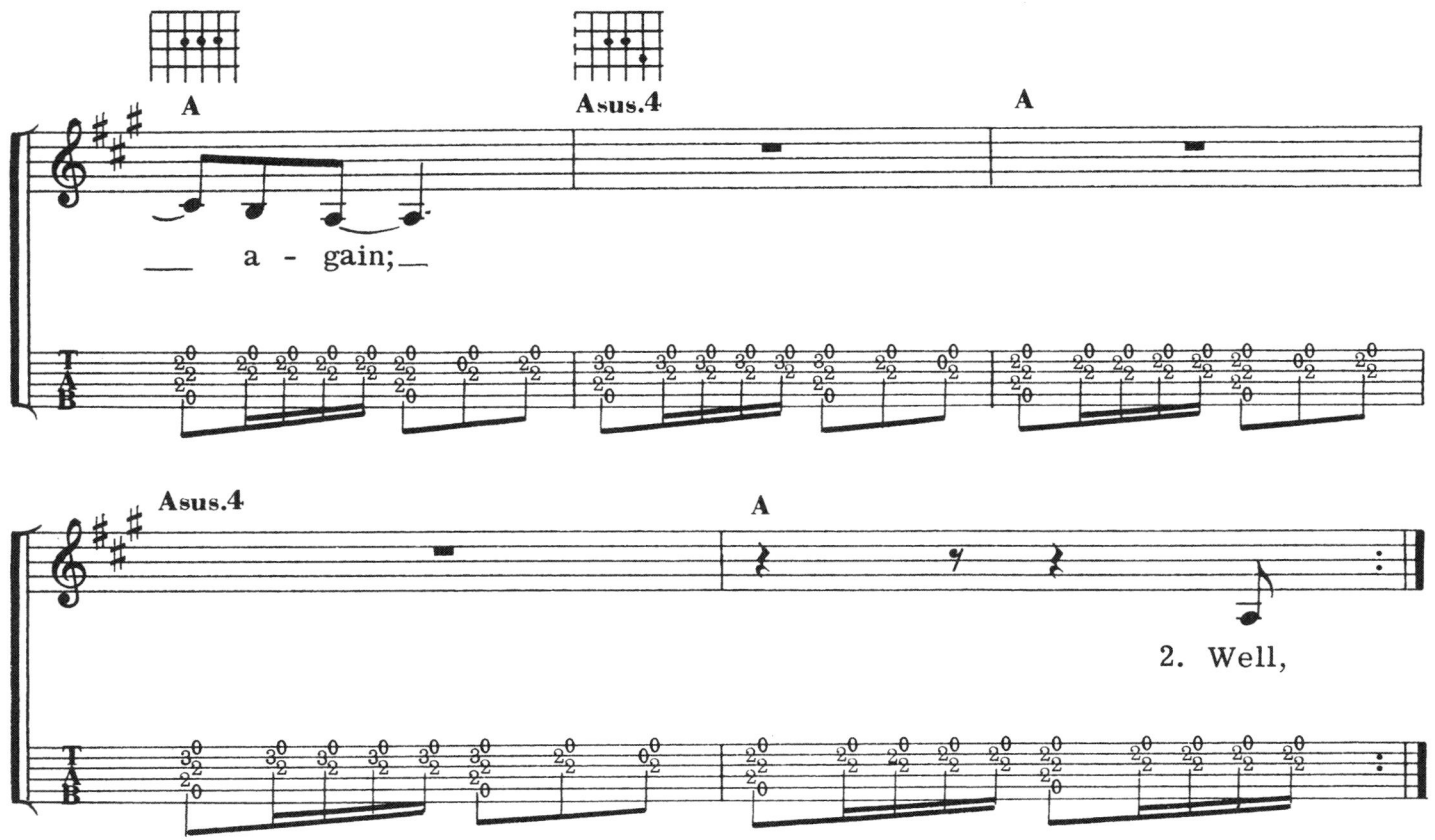

Come over to the window my little darling
I'd like to try to read your palm
I used to think I was some sort of gypsy boy
Before I let you take me home.

CHORUS:
So long, Marianne, it's time that we began
To laugh and cry and laugh about it all again.

Well, you know that I love to live with you
But you make me forget so very much
I forget to pray for the angel
And then the angels forget to pray for us.

We met when we were almost young
Deep in the green lilac park
You held on to me like I was a crucifix
As we went kneeling through the dark.

Your letters they all say that you're beside
  me now
Then why do I feel alone?
I'm standing on a ledge and your fine
  spider web
Is fastening my ankle to a stone.

For now I need your hidden love
I'm cold as a new razor blade
You left when I told you I was curious
I never said that I was brave.

Oh, you are really such a pretty one
I see you've gone and changed your
  name again
And just when I climbed this whole
  mountainside
To wash my eyelids in the rain.

O your eyes, well, I forget your eyes
Your body's at home in every sea
How come you gave away your news
  to everyone
That you said was a secret for me.

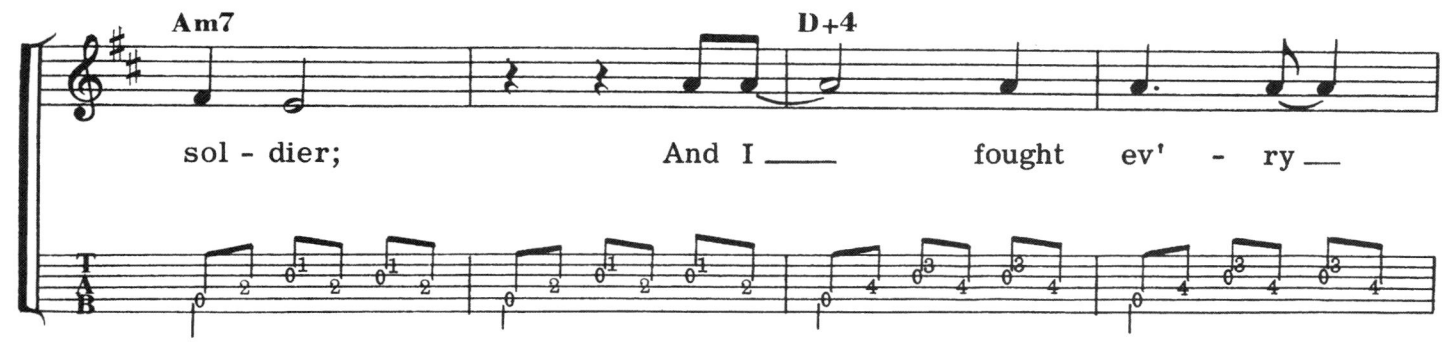

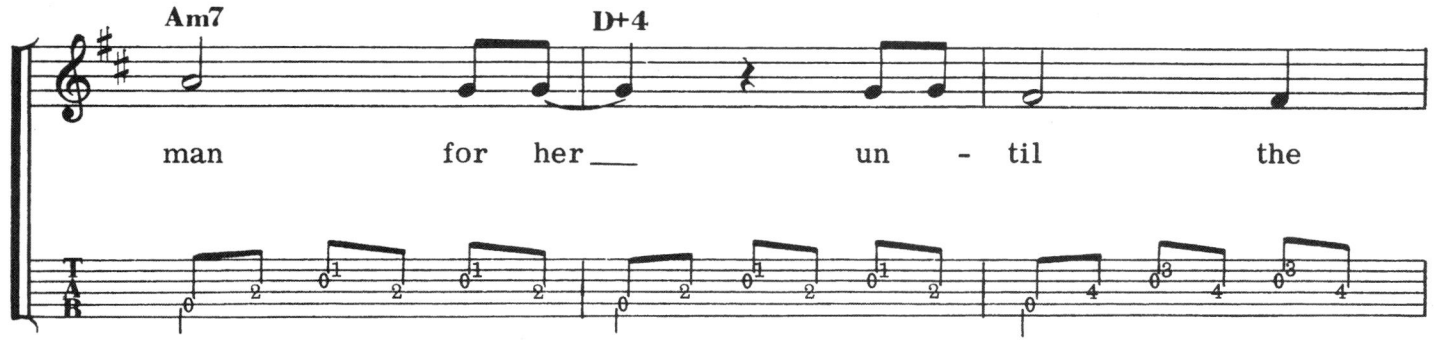

Trav'ling lady stay awhile
Until the night is over
I'm just a station on your way
I know I am not your lover.
    Well I lived with a child of snow
    When I was a soldier
    And I fought ev'ry man for her
    Until the nights grew colder.

Trav'ling lady, stay awhile
Until the night is over
I'm just a station on your way
I know I'm not your lover.

She used to wear her hair like you
Except when she was sleeping
And then she'd weave it on a loom
Of smoke and gold and breathing.
    And why are you so quiet now
    Standing there in the doorway?
    You chose your journey long before
    You came upon this highway.

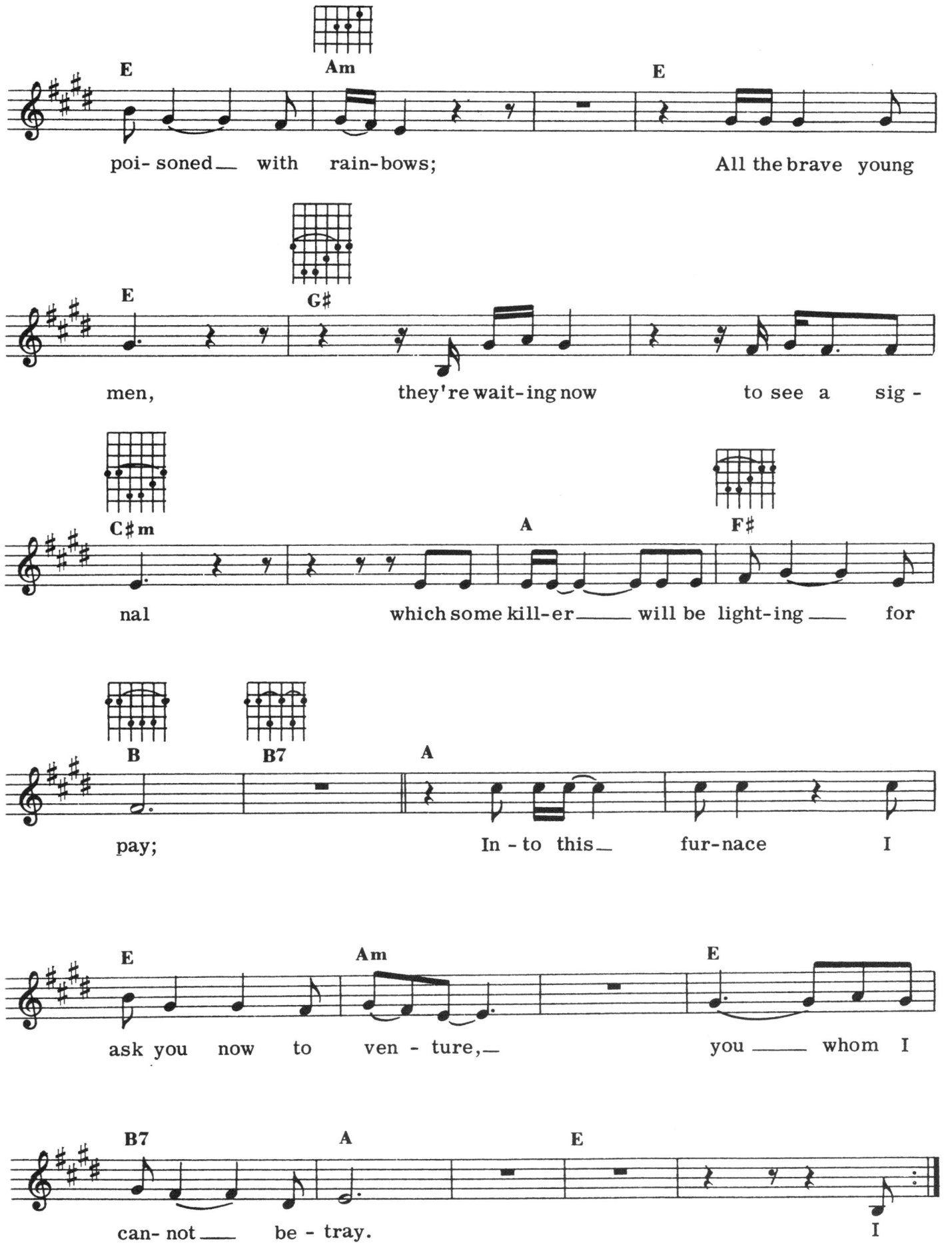

THE OLD REVOLUTION

I finally broke into prison
I found my place in the chain
Even damnation is poisoned with rainbows
All the brave young men they're waiting now to see a signal
Which some killer will be lighting for pay
    Into this furnace I ask you now to venture
    You whom I cannot betray.

I fought in the old revolution
On the side of the ghost and the king
Of course I was very young and I thought that we were winning
I can't pretend I still feel very much like singing
As they carry the bodies away.
    Into this furnace I ask you now to venture
    You whom I cannot betray.

Lately you've started to stutter
As though you had nothing to say
To all of my architects let me be traitor
Now let me say I myself gave the order
To sleep and to search and to destroy.
    Into this furnace I ask you now to venture
    You whom I cannot betray.

You who are broken by power
You who are absent all day
You who are kings for the sake of your childrens' story
The hand of your beggar is burdened down with money
The hand of your lover is clay.
    Into this furnace I ask you now to venture
    You whom I cannot betray.

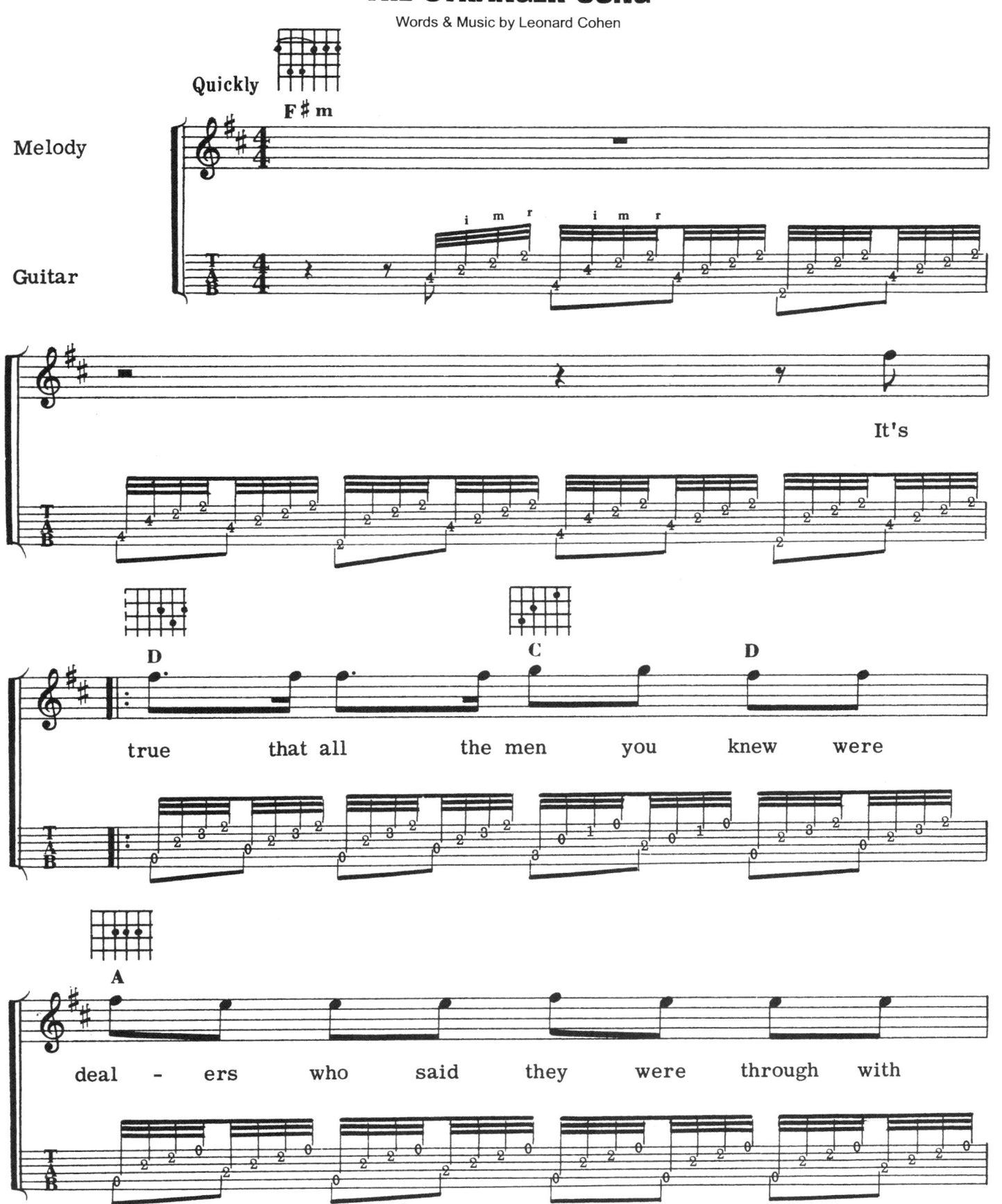

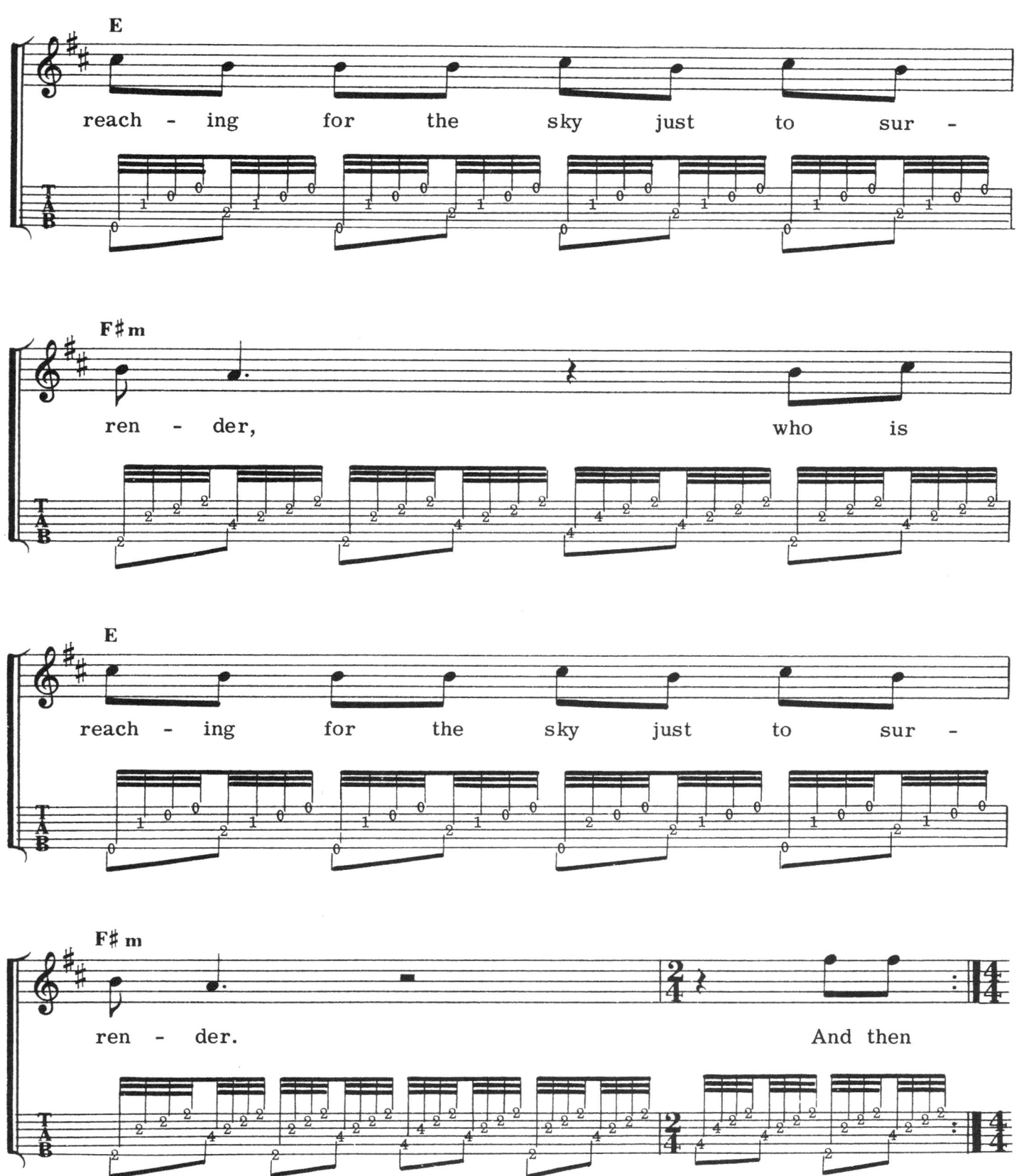

THE STRANGER SONG

It's true that all men you knew
Were dealers who said they were through
With dealing every time you gave them shelter
I know that kind of man
It's hard to hold the hand of anyone
Who's reaching for the sky just to surrender.
Who's reaching for the sky just to surrender.

And then sweeping up the jokers that
   he left behind
You find he did not leave you very much
Not even laughter
Like any dealer, he was watching for the card
   that is so high and wild
He'll never need to deal another
He was just some Joseph looking for a
   manger
He was just some Joseph looking for a
   manger.

And then leaning on your window sill
He'll say one day you caused his will
To weaken with your love and warmth
   and shelter
And then taking from his wallet
   an old schedule of trains, he'll say,
"I told you when I came I was a stranger,
I told you when I came I was a stranger."

But now another stranger
Seems to want to ignore his dreams
As though they were the burden of some other
O, you've seen that kind of man before
His golden arm dispatching cards
But now it's rusted from the elbow to
   the finger
Yes, he wants to trade the game he knows
   for shelter.

You hate to watch another tired man
   lay down his hand, like he was
   giving up the holy game of poker
And while he talks his dreams to sleep
You notice there's a highway that is
   curling up like smoke above his shoulder,
It's curling up like smoke above his shoulder.

You tell him to come in sit down
But something makes you turn around
The door is open, you can't close your shelter
You try the handle of the road
It opens, do not be afraid
It's you my love, you who are the stranger
It is you my love, you who are the stranger.

Well, I've been waiting, I was sure
We'd meet between the trains we're waiting for
I think it's time to board another
Please understand, I never had a secret chart
To get me to the heart
Of this or any other matter
When he talks like this
   you don't know what he's after
When he speaks like this
   you don't know what he's after.

Let's meet tomorrow, if you choose,
Upon the shore, beneath the bridge
That they are building on some endless river
Then he leaves the platform
For the sleeping car that's warm, you realize
He's only advertising one more shelter
And it comes to you, he never was a stranger
And you say, "Ok, the bridge or someplace later."

And then sweeping up the jokers that
   he left behind
You find he did not leave you very much
Not even laughter
Like any dealer, he was watching for the card
   that is so high and wild
He'll never need to deal another
He was just some Joseph looking for a
   manger
He was just some Joseph looking for a
   manger.

And then leaning on your window sill
He'll say one day you caused his will
To weaken with your love and warmth
   and shelter
And then taking from his wallet
   an old schedule of trains, he'll say,
"I told you when I came I was a stranger,
I told you when I came I was a stranger."

wine and bread?

I believe that you heard your master sing
When I was sick in bed
I suppose that he told you everything
That I keep locked away in my head
Your master took you traveling
Well at least that's what you said
And now do you come back to bring
Your prisoner wine and bread?

You met him at some temple
Where they take your clothes at the door
He was just a numberless man in a chair
Who had just come back from the war
And you wrap up his tired face in your hair
And he hands you the apple core
Then he touches your lips, now so suddenly bare
Of all the kisses we put on sometime before.

And he gave you a German shepard to walk
With a collar of leather and nails
And he never once made you explain or talk
About all of the little details
Such as who had a worm and who had a rock
And who had you through the mails
Now your love is a secret all over the block
And it never stops not even
    when your master fails.

He took you up in his aeroplane
Which he flew without any hands
And you cruised above the ribbons of rain
That drove the crowd from the stands
Then he killed the lights in a lonely lane
Where an ape with angel glands
Erased the final wisps of pain
With the music of rubber bands.

And now I hear your master sing
You kneel for him to come
His body is a golden string
That your body is hanging from
His body is a golden string
My body has grown numb
O now you hear your master sing
Your shirt is all undone.

And will you kneel beside this bed
That we polished so long ago
Before your master chose instead
To make my bed of snow?
Your eyes are wild and your knuckles are red
And you're speaking far too low
I can't make out what your master said
Before he made you go.

And I think you're playing far too rough
For a lady who's been to the moon
I've lain by this window long enough
You get used to an empty room
And your love is some dust
In an old man's cuff
Who is tapping his foot to a tune
And your thighs are a ruin
And you want too much
Let's say you came back sometime too soon.

I loved your master perfectly
I taught him all that he knew
He was starving in some deep mystery
Like a man who is sure what is true
And I sent you to him with my guarantee
I could teach him something new
And I taught him how you would long for me
No matter what he said, no matter what you do.

I believe that you heard your master sing
While I was sick in bed
I'm sure that he told you everything
I must keep locked away in my head
Your master took you traveling
Well, at least that's what you said
And now do you come back to bring
Your prisoner wine and bread?

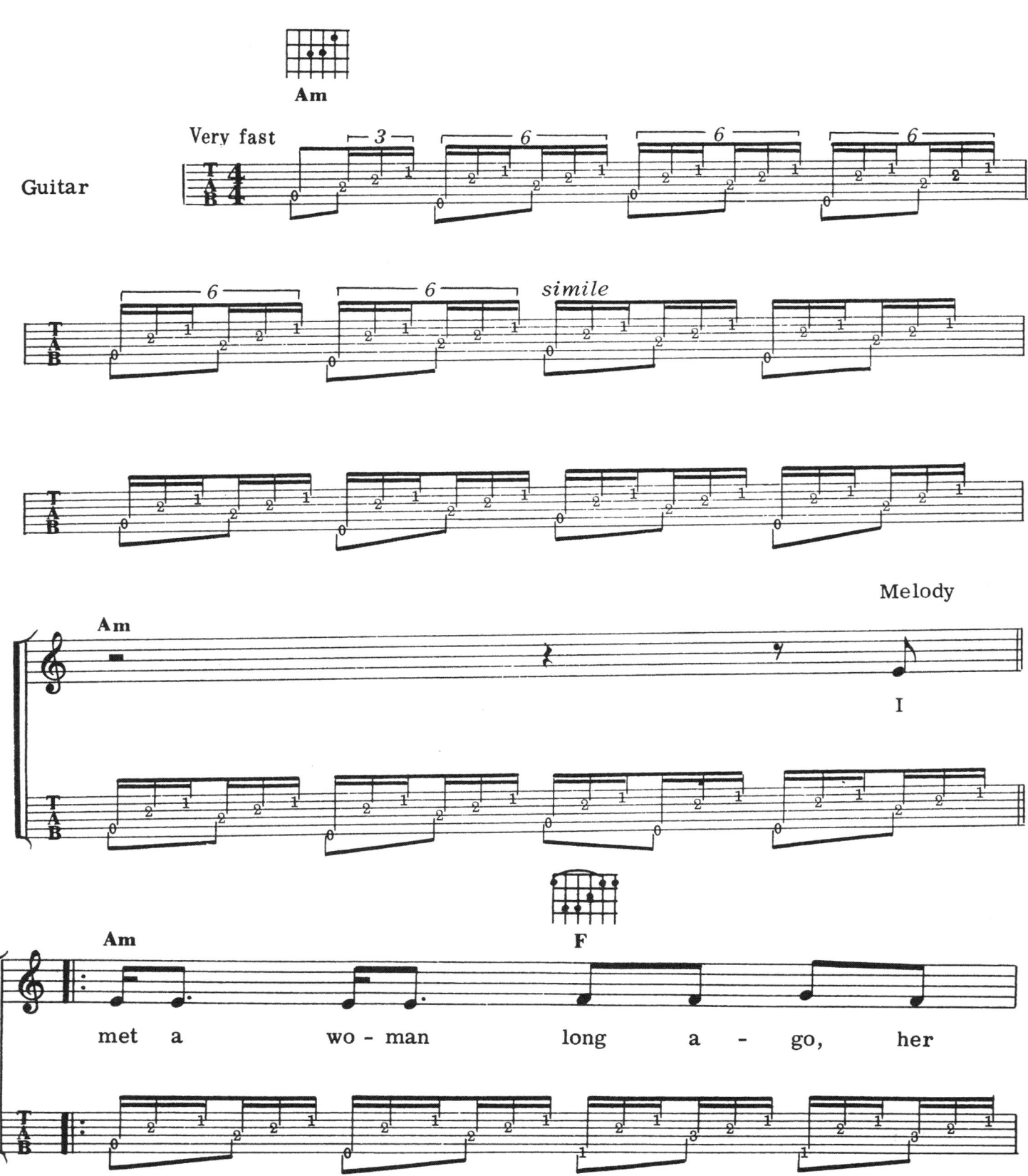

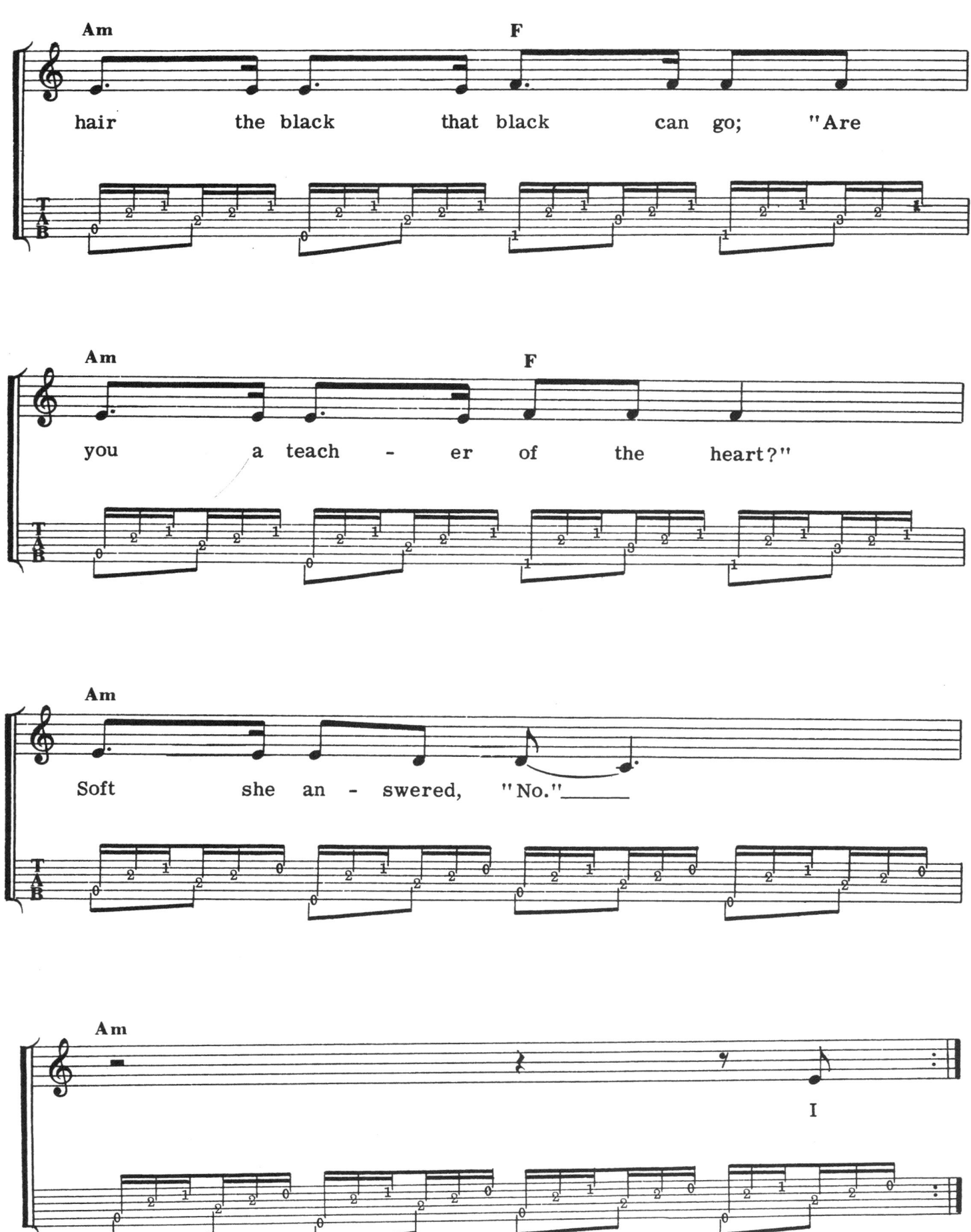

TEACHERS

I met a woman long ago
Her hair the black that black can go
"Are you a teacher of the heart?"
Soft she answered, "No."

I met a girl across the sea
Her hair the gold that gold can be;
"Are you a teacher of the heart?"
"Yes, but not for thee."

I met a man who lost his mind
In some lost place I had to find;
"Follow me," the wise man said
But he walked behind.

I walked into a hospital
Where none was sick and none was well
When at night the nurses left
I could not walk at all.

Morning came and then came noon
Dinner time, a scalpel blade
Lay beside
My silver spoon.

Some girls wander by mistake
Into the mess that scalpels make
"Are you the teachers of my heart?"
"We teach old hearts to break."

One morning I woke up alone
The hospital, the nurses gone
"Have I carved enough, my lord?"
"Child, you are a bone."

I ate and ate and ate
No, I did not miss a plate
"Well, how much do these suppers cost?"
"We'll take it out in hate."

I spent my hatred every place
On every work, on every face
Someone gave me wishes
And I wished for an embrace.

Several girls embraced me, then
I was embraced by men,
"Is my passion perfect?"
"No, do it once again."

I was handsome, I was strong
I knew the words of every song
"Did my singing please you?"
"No, the words you sang were wrong."

Who is it whom I address?
Who takes down what I confess?
"Are you the teachers of my heart?"
"We teach old hearts to rest."

"Teachers, are my lessons done?
I cannot do another one."
They laughed and laughed and said
"Well, child, are your lessons done?
Are your lessons done?
Are your lessons done?"

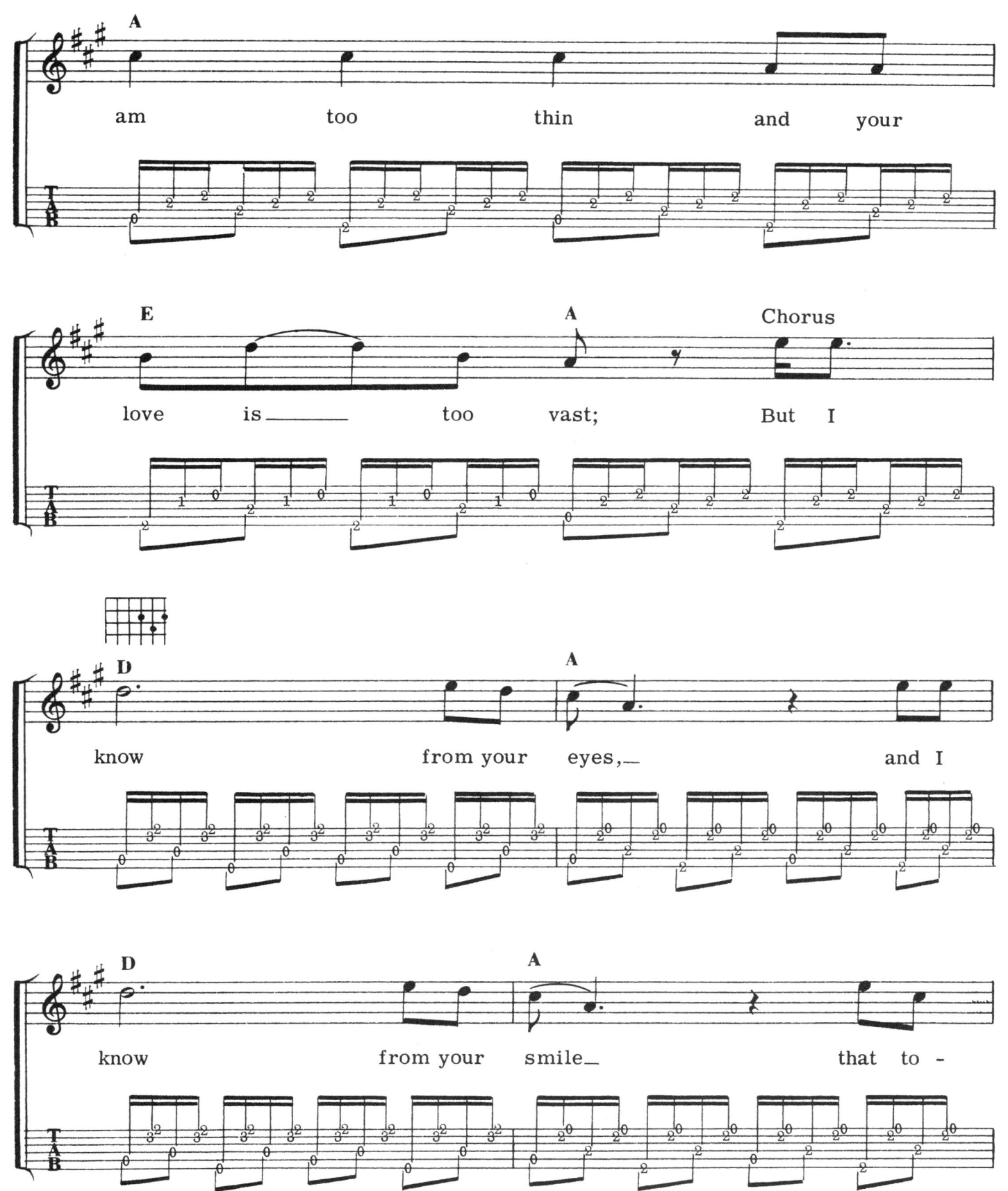

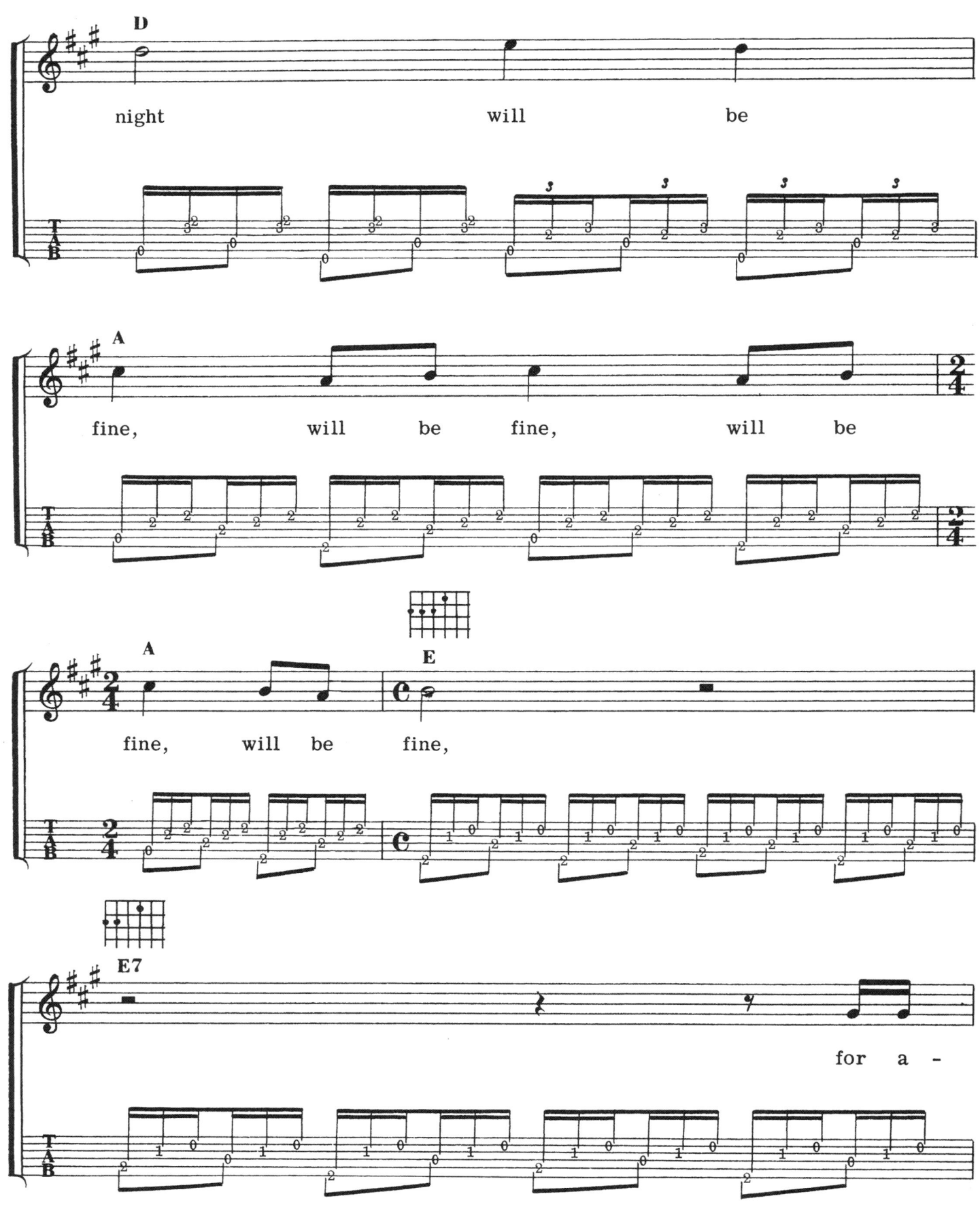

Sometimes I find
I get to thinking of the past,
We swore to each other then
That our love would surely last
You kept right on loving
I went on a fast
Now I am too thin
And your love is too vast.

Chorus (After each verse)
But I know from your eyes
And I know from your smile
That tonight will be fine, will be fine
Will be fine, will be fine for a while.

I choose the rooms
That I live in with care,
The windows are small
And the walls must be bare
There's only one bed
And there's only one prayer
And I listen all night
For your step on the stair.

Sometimes I see her
Undressing for me,
She's the soft naked lady
Love meant her to be
And she's moving her body
So brave and so free.
If I've got to remember
That's a fine memory.

Well, I argued all night like so many have before
Saying, "Whatever you give me I seem to need so much more."
Then she pointed at me where I kneeled on her floor
She said, "Don't try to use me or slyly refuse me
Just win me or lose me, it is this that the darkness is for."

I cried, "Oh, Lady Midnight, I fear that you grow old,
Stars eat your body and the wind makes you cold."
"If we cry now," she said, "It will just be ignored."
So I walked through the morning, the sweet early morning
I could hear my lady calling, "You've won me, you've won me, my lord;"
   "You've won me, you've won me, my lord;"
   "Yes, you've won me, you've won me, my lord."

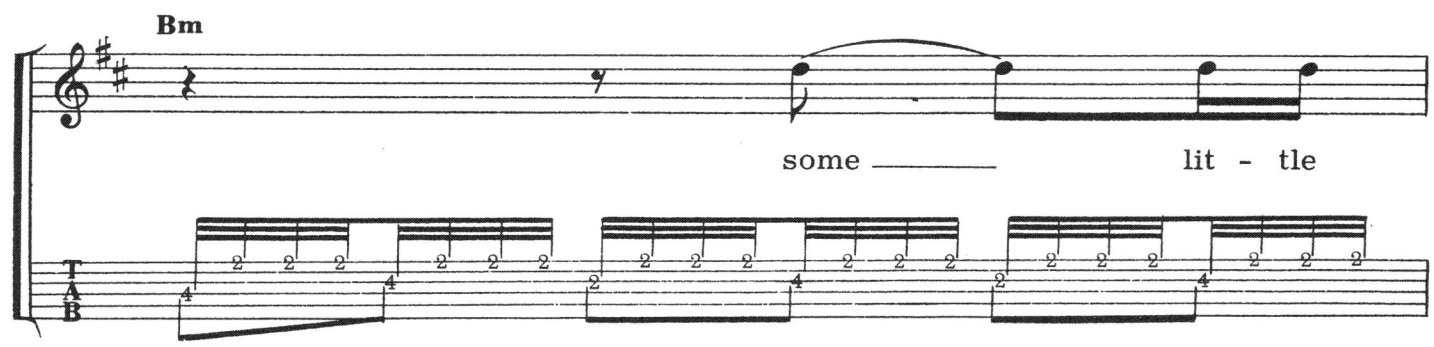

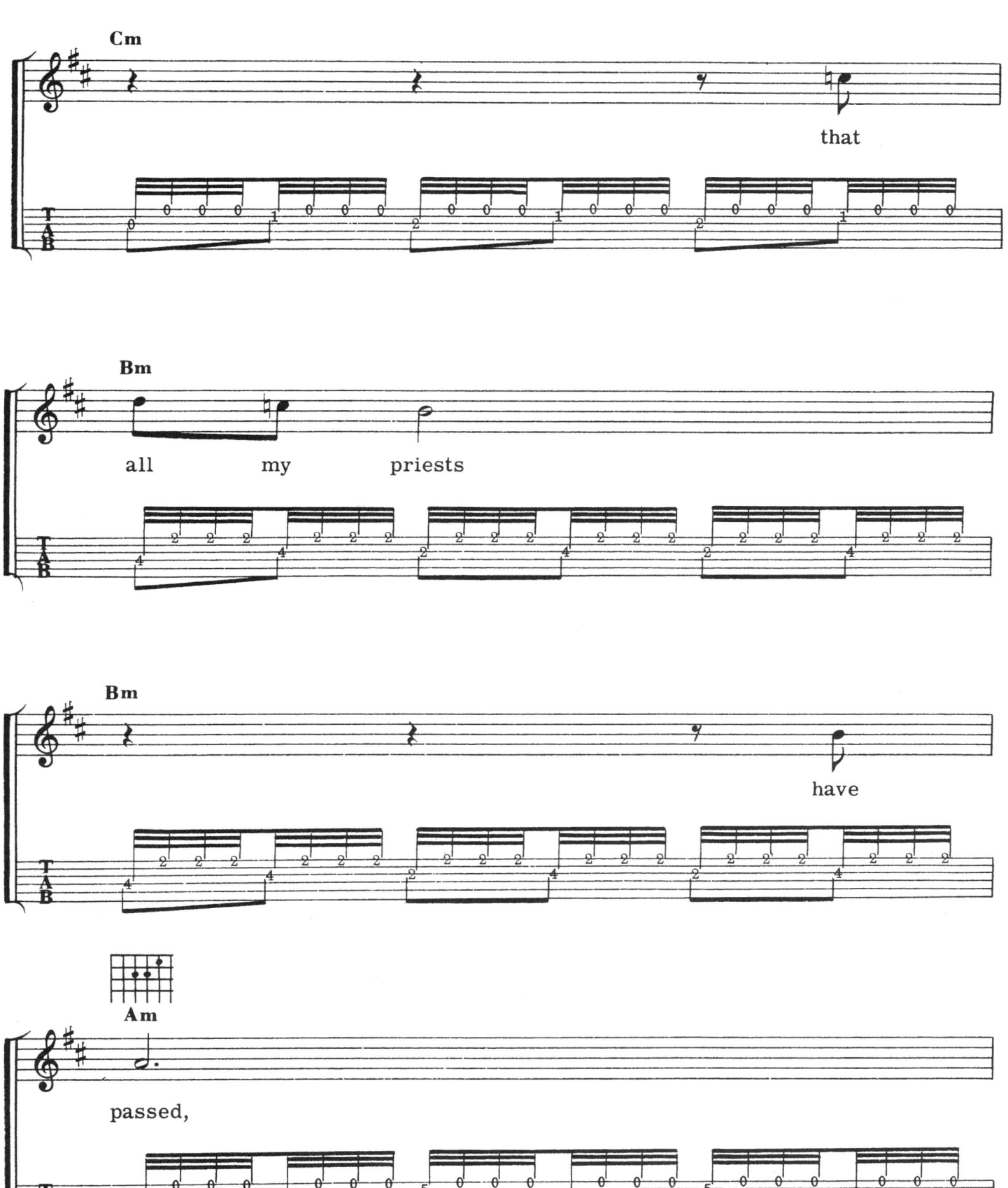

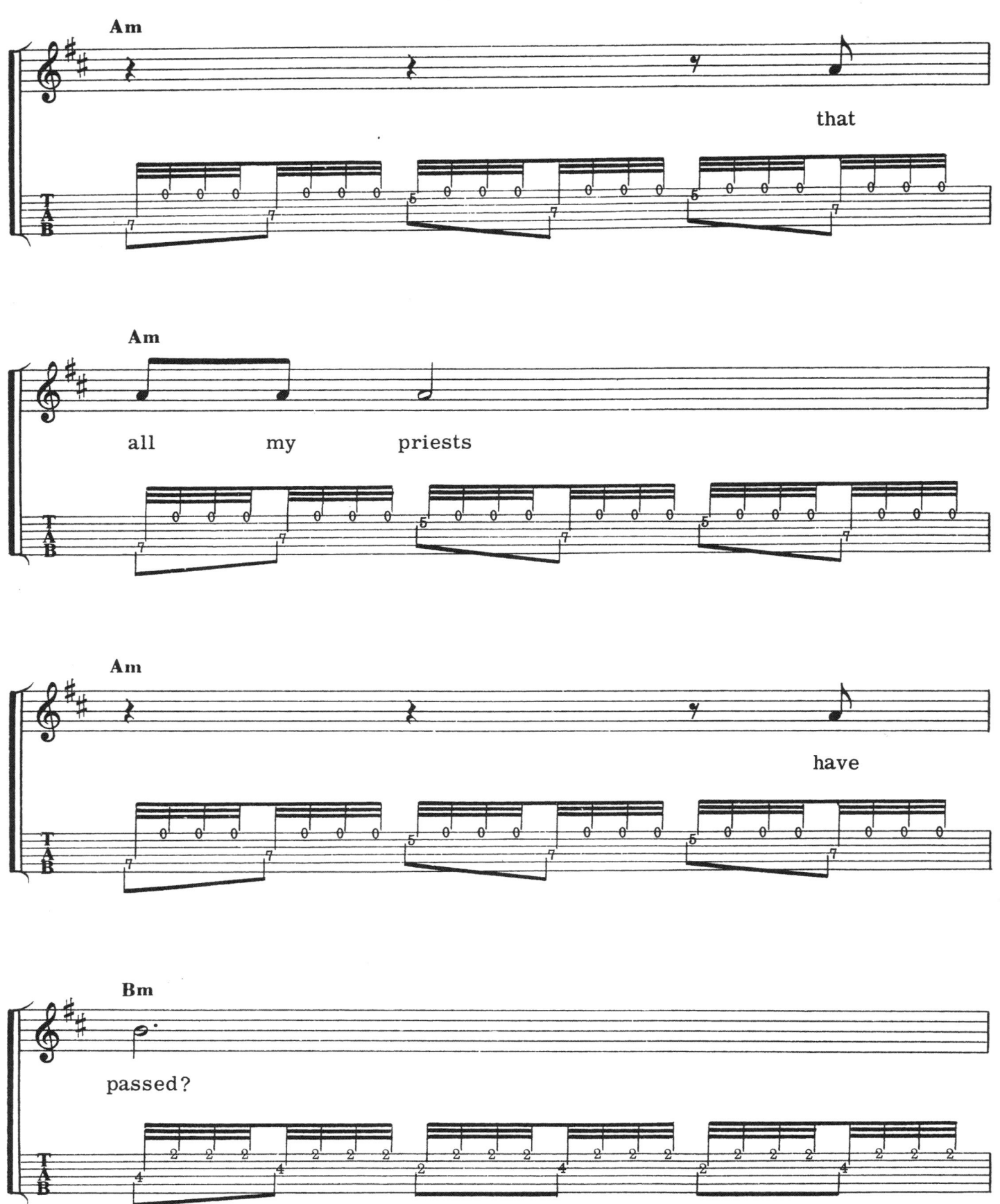

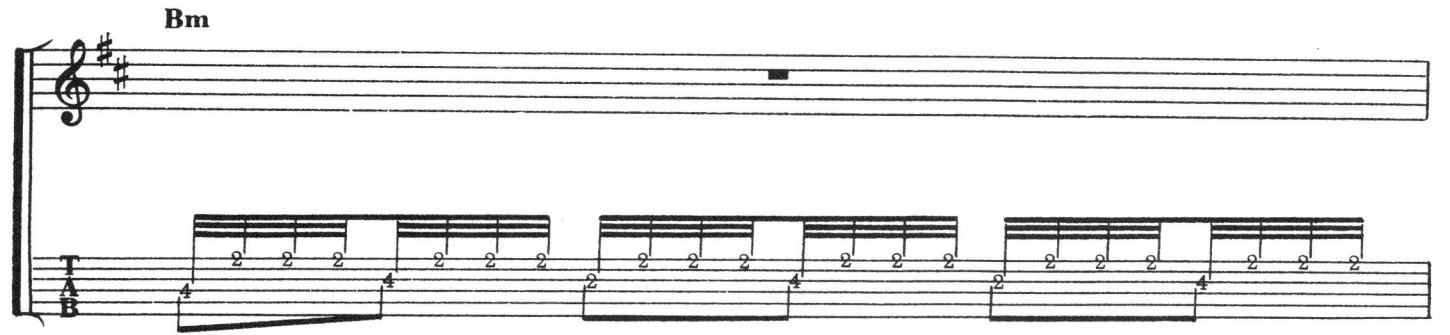

And who will write love songs for you
When I am lord at last
And your body is some little highway shrine
That all my priests have passed
That all my priests have passed.

My priests they will put flowers there
They will stand before the glass
But they'll wear away your little window, love
They will trample on the grass
They will trample on the grass.

And who will aim the arrow
That men will follow through your grace
When I am lord of memory
And all of your armour has turned to lace
And all your armour has turned to lace?

The simple life of heroes
And the twisted life of saints
They just confuse the sunny calendar
With their red and golden paints
With their red and golden paints.

And all of you have seen the dance
That God has kept from me
But He has seen me watching you
When all your minds were free
When all your minds were free.

Repeat verses 1 and 2.

THE BUTCHER

Words & Music by Leonard Cohen

I came upon a butcher
He was slaughtering a lamb
I accused him there
With his tortured lamb
He said "Listen to me, child
I am what I am
And you, you are my only son."

Well, I found a silver needle
I put it into my arm
It did some good
Did some harm.
But the nights were cold
And it almost kept me warm
How some the night is long?

I saw some flowers growing up
Where that lamb fell down
Was I supposed to praise my lord
Make some kind of joyful sound?
He said, "Listen, listen to me now
I go round and round,
And you, you are my only child."

Do not leave me now,
Do not leave me now,
I'm broken down
From a recent fall.
Blood upon my body
And ice upon my soul
Lead on, my son, it is your world.

© Copyright 1969 Sony/ATV Songs LLC, USA.
Chrysalis Songs Limited.
All Rights Reserved. International Copyright Secured.